Because *Kids* Are Worth It!

BY JAKE TERPSTRA

Copyright © 2013 by Jake Terpstra

Because Kids Are Worth It!
by Jake Terpstra

Printed in the United States of America

ISBN 9781626976672

All rights reserved solely by the author. The author guarantees all contents are original and do not infringe upon the legal rights of any other person or work. No part of this book may be reproduced in any form without the permission of the author. The views expressed in this book are not necessarily those of the publisher.

www.xulonpress.com

Foreword

Gary R. Anderson PhD, LMSW
Director, Michigan State University School of Social Work (and former child protective service worker)

This book is full of insight and observations that can guide current policy leaders, agency administrators, university faculty members, and front-line child welfare workers in their professional service and policy-making. The persistent and vexing challenges confronting the field of child welfare are thoughtfully identified and distilled by an expert child welfare professional, Jake Terpstra. He has worked in and observed a range of child welfare programs and policies at the local, state and federal levels over a number of decades and from a variety of relevant vantage points. Thankfully, he reflects on and shares many of the lessons he has learned over these years of service. This familiarity has nurtured a life-long commitment to positive outcomes for children and families and justifiable impatience with the obstacles to effective services. In his many years of experience, he has accumulated a long list of problems with the child welfare system but his many years of service and leadership attest to the ability to make a difference and underscore the potential for improvement and reform.

In chapter one, the historical development and devolution of child welfare services promotes an understanding of the forces and organizations that have shaped and influenced child welfare in America. In chapter two, the introduction of a number of accountability steps illustrates the complexity of the work and the impact of unintended consequences for service delivery. The positive contribution of permanency planning stands out in contrast to other measures that weakened child welfare as described in chapter three and the reductions and losses in the 1980's described in chapter four. In chapter five, the author highlights the crucial role of supervisors and organizational leaders and the exercise of power and the resulting impacts on workers, programs, and agencies. After dissecting the language and words used in child welfare and underscoring the importance of communication, in the final chapters a thoughtful plan for rebuilding child welfare is presented.

Reflecting Jake Terpstra's deep knowledge and extensive experience in child welfare, this book repeatedly and thoroughly hits the mark when analyzing and identifying the problems and in highlighting the small and large steps toward renewal and success. Whether new to child welfare or a veteran of child welfare service provision, this book will increase your knowledge, add to your understanding, and

Foreword

point toward promising actions. Affirming the role of social work, training and workforce development, innovation and leadership, the reader will appreciate the author's dismay with political and programmatic shortcomings but ultimately be encouraged to persist and work toward a better system to more effectively meet the needs of children and families.

Introduction (to Because Kids Are Worth It!)

Each year nearly a quarter of a million children are separated from their families and enter the child welfare system, most of them going into family foster homes. The average amount of time spent there is approximately 27 months. Their experience during that time has a profound effect on them, their descendants and indirectly also on other people in their lives. This book is about the way the system operates.

The cumulative effect of child welfare services on this huge number of people over many years is incalculable. It is obvious that they directly or indirectly impact a substantial portion of the American population and also influence our culture. Relatively few people are in a position to be able to understand the experiences the children have while they are in the system. That generally is kept from public view though not intentionally.

Many people working in child welfare agencies work very hard to make children's experience therapeutic and help them to move on to a better future. At the same time they also face many obstacles which make that difficult.

The information in the book is intended to explain to readers both positive and negative factors that affect those services, especially people who are directly involved. It contains information about the history of child welfare services, beginning in 1854, to the present time. The author relies partly on his own experience in over 50 years of experience in child welfare services on multiple levels including involvement with child welfare personnel first throughout Michigan, then throughout the country. The content includes his observations, experiences and opinions about how child welfare services became what they currently are, with recommendations for improvement.

BECAUSE KIDS ARE WORTH IT!

Foreword. v
Introduction ix
Chapter 1 – Careful Building Takes Time. . . . 13
Chapter 2 – The Decline of Child Welfare Quality . . 21
Chapter 3 – We Also Did It to Ourselves 35
Chapter 4 – The 1980's 53
Chapter 5 – Supervision and Administration. . . 61
Chapter 6 – Semantics 75
Chapter 7 – Rebuilding 85
About the Author 113
Acknowledgements 115

Chapter 1

CAREFUL BUILDING TAKES TIME

"Child welfare service isn't rocket science. It is tougher." Dave Liederman, director of the Child Welfare League of America, made that assertion, and no one questioned it. It should not be so tough; conceptually it is rather clear. So why is it? Many cases are complicated, sometimes intractable, and all are different. Public funds are used for most services and political values change with each administration. Other changes, including internal changes, often have unexpected consequences. All these factors contribute to complexities with which child welfare staff must deal.

"Child welfare" is a term that encompasses services that deal with child abuse and neglect as well as services to prevent removal of the children. If children are removed, they are placed into family foster care and group foster care. Family reunification, adoption and post adoption services may be provided and youth who "age out" of the system are helped to be self-sufficient.

Child welfare, though very complex, can be taught and learned. The content is only a part of the reason why it is tougher than rocket science. The shifting sand, coming from many sources, makes it almost unknowable. How are new caseworkers to work through the maze and understand what it is, what is required, and why? Perhaps the experiences and observations of others may help them to understand the problems and issues. That will not necessarily point to solutions, but understanding history, including cause and effect, also can make the present more understandable and hopefully easier to cope with.

Social work and child welfare were tightly bound from their beginnings. The three main origins of social work are first, private charity programs that were developed in the 19th century, second, the settlement houses for immigrants (especially Hull House in Chicago administered by Jane Adams a pioneer in social work), and third, the Orphan Trains. In this context the Orphan Trains were especially significant because they also were the forerunner of contemporary child welfare service, considered to be a social work function and initially carried out by social workers.

"Orphan trains", which were regular trains, began carrying homeless children from New York to farm families as far west as the railroads existed, eventually to California and western Canada.

Careful Building Takes Time

Initially arrangements were made possible by the efforts of Rev. Charles Loring Brace in New York, who became concerned about hordes of homeless children on the streets of New York and those crowded into orphanages. The conditions of children in orphanages were pathetic, and street children, trying to survive, also could be dangerous, as Brace described in a book, *The Dangerous Classes of New York City*. High immigration, depression and disease epidemics, especially cholera and small pox, were major causes of family breakdown. Brace started the New York Children's Aid Society, which continues to exist, and led the movement to bring over 200,000 children from New York to families in the west from 1854 to 1929.

The families selected for children, brought to their towns in sizeable groups, were put on display in those towns, and families generally could pick the children they wanted. The homes were visited annually by an "agent" who frequently did not see the children or talk with them alone. This rather haphazard system naturally led to very unfortunate arrangements, as well as good selections with positive outcomes. It is estimated that there now are over four million descendants of those "riders." The term "agency" originated with this arrangement.

Until that time conditions for parentless children were abysmal, including indenture, imprisonment with adults for older children, as well as confinement in asylums. Mortality rates in some children's hospitals approached 100%.

Because Kids Are Worth It!

Although the orphan train program was highly flawed, it improved conditions for nearly all the children it placed. However the major contribution was that until then orphanage care was considered appropriate, in fact almost automatic, for homeless children, and the program shifted national values away from orphanage care to family care as basic for children's needs.

More children enter the child welfare system annually now than were placed in the 75 years that the orphan trains operated.

Social work originated at the turn of the 20th century, and gradually became the professional service responsible for child welfare. This included services for children separated from their families throughout the country.

The U. S. Children's Bureau was signed into law by President Taft on April 9, 1912. The initial mandate of the legislation was: "The said bureau shall investigate and report to the Department of Commerce and Labor upon all matters pertaining to the welfare of children and child life among all classes of people, and shall especially investigate the questions of mortality, the birth rate, orphanage, juvenile courts, desertion, dangerous occupations, accidents, and diseases of children, employment, legislation affecting children in the several states and territories."

Children's Bureau funds established by the Social Security Act in 1935 have gone to public and private institutions of higher learning to train social workers and others, with special emphasis on child welfare.

Research and training grants also have been used to support and expand knowledge in such areas as protective services for neglected and abused children, day care and foster care services, adoption services, environmental effects on children's development and services to unmarried parents. Children's Bureau staff who specialized in various types of service, including those listed above, also provided consultation and training to agencies throughout the country.

In 1920 the Child Welfare League of America was established. It is a voluntary, constituent-supported organization. Its primary mission has been to raise standards of child welfare services in the United States and to assist member agencies. While CWLA's services primarily were directed to private agencies, the Children's Bureau programs were directed primarily to public services. However there also was a great deal of cooperative effort and the organizations have a rich history of collaboration to maximize their effectiveness. These two organizations continue to provide leadership and support to the field until the present time.

Much of the base of child welfare services originated in *Parens patriae*, part of English common law developed in the 16th century. It grants the state power to protect individuals who lack the capacity to act in their own interests, giving the state power to intervene to protect children when their parents fail to do so.

Child welfare services in the U.S. continued to be supported primarily by private charity until enactment of the Social Security Act of 1935 which allocated public funds for administering child welfare services and for training social work staff. Nearly all subsequent Federal child welfare legislation amends the Social Security Act. World War II slowed development of services, but social work became firmly established as the professional foundation of child welfare in the 1940s and 50s. Other professional services, e.g. law, engineering, teaching and medicine, also have a professional and academic base where services, academia and professional organizations work hand-in-hand.

This was true of child welfare in the middle of last century, with agencies having strong connections with the National Association of Social Workers (NASW), schools of social work and the Council on Social Work Education (CSWE). Each of these worked cooperatively to contribute to the field from its perspective. Significantly, child welfare became the only service that is a social service carried out primarily with social work concepts and administered by social workers. Conversely, the profession of social work has only one "child", child welfare. As the profession of social work became more generally recognized, it was considered the appropriate discipline for carrying out child welfare services.

The federal government increased funding for training and participated in child welfare conferences. The premier conferences throughout most of the last century were White House Conferences on Children and Youth, held once a decade. They brought together leaders from all segments of child welfare, and produced recommendations that were

Careful Building Takes Time

used for administrative policy development and for drafting legislation. They also helped to serve as a cushion between agencies serving children and politics, which sometimes has other priorities. Political interests are not necessarily in the best interests of children, but the conferences helped to bring them together. The White House Conferences for Children were initiated by President Theodore Roosevelt in 1909 and ended by President Reagan in 1980.

During the decades immediately after World War II, child welfare gained new footing and also was conceptualized more clearly, developing nationwide consistency. Much of this was the result of efforts of schools of social work, which worked closely with child welfare agencies to provide leadership and training, while at the same time constantly learning from the field what staff training needs were, and incorporating them into curriculums. This on-going network was mutually beneficial. The Child Welfare League of America and the U.S. Children's Bureau also were active partners in that effort.

During that era, state child welfare services were administered by a separate department in each state or by relatively independent divisions within other departments, often departments of public welfare. The educational norm for child welfare line staff was at least one year of graduate school training, while supervisors and administrators had Master's degrees in social work.

Does this suggest that child welfare was all that it could be? Of course not, it had many flaws. A major one was that permanency planning concepts were

Because Kids Are Worth It!

just beginning to be developed, with many children still being allowed to drift in limbo care sometimes for many years. The number of children in out-of-home care grew to well over a half million by the 1970s. Nevertheless, from that time, child welfare services deteriorated, and people sometimes ask if there ever was a golden age. The response of those who lived through that time could be, "No, but that was as close as we ever came. And it was more like it than anything we have seen since."

> Many things can wait. Children cannot.
> Today their bones are being formed,
> their blood is being made,
> and their senses are being developed.
> To them we cannot say tomorrow.
> Their name is today.

Chapter 2

THE DECLINE OF CHILD WELFARE

The century-long development of contemporary child welfare was a very slow process. In retrospect it may appear to be a relatively steady process, even though it was a difficult time with setbacks and uneven gains as a result of recognized needs and efforts of relatively few people. Writers, such as social worker Homer Folks, 1867-1963, left extensive writings about much of this period. However, as the highlights mentioned in the previous chapter indicate, progress continued throughout that period.

Dismantling is a much faster process than building, whether it is done to programs or buildings. The last half century has been a mix of both, with a general decline in service quality and steep increases in costs. Some of the major negative factors were imposed on child welfare from outside itself. That does not suggest that there also were not negative influences originating inside the system. Howeve, they will be subjects of subsequent chapters.

In the late 1950s public welfare programs were struggling with blending responsibility for determining public assistance client eligibility and providing direct services for them. Gradually it seemed clear that those functions should be administered separately if each was to be effective. Then the expression "When the pendulum swings, it swings exceedingly far" became reality. If there is a phenomenon that has plagued child welfare throughout this period, it is extreme pendulum swings. Changes, like this one, often were extreme, with consequences worse than the circumstances they were intended to correct.

In the mid-1960s when administrators of the federal Department of Health, Education and Welfare (later changed to the Department of Health and Human Services by President Carter) concluded that the separation of eligibility determination and service functions was needed. The change that was mandated went far beyond simply separating them. The planners believed that combining services in the public assistance programs primarily for adults and those in child welfare could be more efficiently administered together. The mandate was that both service categories be administered in a "single organizational unit" (SOU). The result was an example of unintended consequences. This action caused administrative changes in state and county child welfare programs throughout the country. State and county public assistance agencies were larger than child welfare programs, and the child welfare services, being smaller, were subsumed into those programs.

The consequence was that child welfare services were no longer identifiable entities and lost their social work administrative leadership. The carefully nurtured connections with schools of social work also were lost. Gradually child welfare content in university curriculums was eliminated. This led to a double-sided consequence: many administrators did not understand the value of social work education for social workers. Within a decade only one-fourth of child welfare staff throughout the country had *any* child welfare education, while school of social work curriculums lost child welfare content.

In very recent years the number of staff with social work training increased to 40 percent as a result of federal Title IV E training funds. Child welfare content in university curriculums, however, still is insufficient.

There were exceptions to the organizational change however. States were permitted to request waivers to the SOU, and three did (Connecticut, Illinois and Oregon) which kept child welfare services separate. From the perspective of staff of the U.S. Children's Bureau, the quality of those child welfare services continued for some time, while they did not in the other states. In recent years most states have again developed departments for child and family services, or identifiable units within departments, because the complexity of these services requires leadership that can focus on child welfare services without also having to administer unrelated programs.

With de-professionalization of child welfare, described above, it was not long before service quality began to diminish, predictably resulting in well publicized tragedies. Then people in position to make decisions began a long process of adding "accountability" measures to the functions of child welfare staff. Detailed case recording also was increased. Generally these measures were based on reasonable concepts, but their total cumulative negative affect on direct services was not understood. Each new accountability "fix" increased the workload of child welfare staff.

One of these "remedies" was foster care review boards (FCRB) which review cases, selected either by special request, or when statistical reports indicate that children's cases are not progressing, or by special request. Foster parents can request reviews if they feel that cases are not handled properly.

My three- year experience on a FCRB revealed a surprising amount of problematic case handling even by agencies that maintain a positive public image. Their staff usually put considerable time into preparing for the reviews and presenting the cases. One of the disconcerting aspects of the experience was the frequency of workers saying the case was new to them, though not necessarily to the agency, or that another worker had left and they were temporarily covering the case. It usually was not clear whether this was the result of frequent staff turnover, or of agency juggling caseloads for internal reasons.

The Decline of Child Welfare

Review board reviews often led to better services for the reviewed cases, but not necessarily to the quality of agency services

When judges observed that many children needed more attention than caseworkers were able to provide, court appointed special advocates (CASA) program was developed. These advocates are people who volunteer to the court to be a special friend and advocate for a particular child. This was intended to raise the quality of the experience of children in foster care. There is little question about this being true for individual children. Child welfare staff, however, often are not enthusiastic about them, because they generally do not talk with the worker about the child, and consequently do not know what the child's case plan is and are not able to support it with the child. Staff also are concerned when a CASA worker gives special favors and gifts to "their" child, when there also may be other children in the home, who then feel neglected even more. This role conflict can trigger strong personal feelings. Several CASA volunteers presented at the FCRB where I served. Each time we were impressed with the quality of the individuals and their knowledge about the child with whom they worked. However it also raised the question of whether caseworkers would like very much to be able to do what the volunteers do, but do not have time, while little attention is paid to their needs.

State ombudsman programs were designed to help resolve differences and conflicts, but have become highly formalized and preparing for them can be an extremely cumbersome, expensive and time-consuming process for staff.

As a result, relatively few cases can be reviewed and hopefully resolved.

State and federal audits and reviews are frequent, absorbing a great deal of staff time. Federal Child and Family Services Review (FCFSR) reviews have the potential of reducing federal funds if services do not meet requirements. However, when fund shortages contributed to the program deficiencies in the first place the state has been placed in double jeopardy. It also is recognized that there also have been considerable program improvements resulting from these reviews.

As requirements for information from various sources grew, proliferation of reports, and the number of reporting forms also grew, with staff being required to complete all of them. Staff report that 50 to 75 percent of their time is used for "paperwork." A profound irony is that the relationship of the child and the caseworker is the essence or "stock in trade", of child welfare. The system has made staff-child relationships difficult, even when caseloads are reasonable. The proliferation of reporting requirements for caseworkers illustrates the applicability of an adage from medical services that "The chart is not the patient."

Deinstitutionalization was like a tidal wave that swept the country in the early 1970s. Though the movement was primarily in the mental health field, it had a profound effect on child welfare. When inadequacies in state mental hospitals and state schools for mentally challenged ("retarded") persons received sufficient negative publicity, the decision was made to close them. Again an all-or-nothing approach prevailed. The objective was based on the assumption that community services would be developed to meet the needs of the thousands of people released from the large state institutions.

When plans were made to close the Plymouth State Home and Training School in Michigan, I was asked to head a committee to meet with parents and their children to help prepare them for the children's return. We met many times and the interviews seemed successful. However my recommendation was that a small group care program be maintained as a back-up arrangement for the children whose families would not able to care for them adequately, to expedite planning for alternatives. Though it was not accepted then, later a new group care facility was developed for that purpose.

The anticipated community services were not developed as expected, with negative consequences for many people and problems for communities. Many children in need of mental health services or special education entered the child welfare system, requiring major program changes and complicating staff responsibilities. Another consequence of deinstitutionalization is that now prisons are used for mentally ill people without adequate therapeutic services for them. Current estimates of persons in prison with mental health needs run as high as 40 percent. Simultaneously, the number of homeless people rose dramatically, apparently because many of the mentally challenged people were not able to cope, and community programs were scarce. Homelessness was rare prior to that time.

Some of the children who had been in those programs entered the child welfare system and their needs probably were better cared for, but services also became more complex.

Perhaps the greatest change in child welfare in recent decades is increased involvement of courts. As inadequacies in the system became more apparent, it was assumed that people's rights and interests were not well protected and case plans were not implemented promptly. While that was accurate, the issue also was much larger; case assessment and therefore also case planning had become inadequate. The Adoption and Child Welfare Act of 1980 required that a court or the agency to review the status of a child in any non-permanent child care setting every six months to determine what is in the best interests of the child, with emphasis on returning a child home as soon as feasible, requiring the court or administrative body to determine the child's future status, whether it is return to parents, adoption, or continued foster care, within 18 months after initial placement into foster care. While case reviews were required, agencies had the option of arranging internal reviews or having cases reviewed by courts.

The Adoption and Safe Families Act, an amendment to the Social Security Act, requires (1) the court or agency review the status of a child in any non-permanent child-care setting every six months to determine the best interests of the child, with most emphasis on returning the child to the home as soon as feasible This Act (2) requires that the court or administrative body determine the child's future status, whether it is return to parents, adoption or continued foster care, within 18 months after initial placement into foster care. (3) Case reviews were required, giving agencies the option of arranging internal reviews or having cases reviewed by courts. (4) Permanency hearings were required to be held no later than 12 months after the child enters foster care. (5) States were mandated to initiate TPR (termination of parental rights) proceedings after the child has been in foster care 15 of the previous 22 months, except if termination was not in the best interest of the child, or if the child is in the care of a relative.

Another amendment to the Social Security Act, the Deficit Reduction Act of 2005 required courts and agencies to demonstrate meaningful collaboration in child welfare proceedings, permitted states to allow public access to certain court child welfare proceedings and provides for the training of judges, attorneys and other legal personnel through improvement grants.

The Child and Family Improvement Act of 2006 reauthorized and extended the Court Improvement Program through FY 2011.

The original purpose of these three acts was to require that children in foster care be moved efficiently toward permanence, which generally is reunification or adoption. However, with each of these legislative acts the role of the courts was increased and control of the child welfare agencies over their cases reduced.

Though intended to improve services for children and their families, by shoring up those services, increased court involvement also brought unintended consequences. Child welfare services became more litigious, requiring more time-consuming paper work. With both these factors operating, child welfare gradually moved toward being a legalistic program rather than a social service. Opposing parties in cases often each have a lawyer. Some judges virtually supervise caseworkers, making decisions formerly considered administrative and supervisory. In my foster care review board experience it was normal to see more lawyers than social workers

The Federal law described above is clear about which organization has responsibility regarding case handling. The law, in Sec 471 (a) (2) states, "such child's placement and care are the responsibility of (A) the State agency administering the state plan approved under Section 471, or (B) any other public agency with whom the State agency administering or supervising the administration of the State plan approved under Section 471 has made an agreement which still is in effect." This mandate generally is not carried out. Instead cases often are handled as though courts are responsible for case planning as well as protection of legal rights.

A simple exercise can help to put the hierarchy of current roles into perspective. In cases involving school age children, with the question, "Who in the system knows the most about the child?" Normally it can be expected to be as follows:

1. the child
2. the child's parents
3. foster parents
4. the caseworker
5. the caseworker's supervisor
6. the child's lawyer or the guardian ad litem
7. the judge

However, the ranking of who has the most authority is the opposite. Next, the question of whose life is most affected by the court decisions shows the same ranking as the first list. It changes again with the question of who is paid the most for the time they are involved?

Role conflict can be a concern in organizations. With legislation involving child welfare and its application, it is surprising that organizational roles were never defined by Congress, the courts or the Federal agency. The proper role of the agency, which is in the administrative executive branch of government, and the role of the court, which is in the judicial branch of government, has not been examined by organizations in a position to do that. The issue of constitutional separation of powers between branches of government does not receive scrutiny regarding the way those roles play out in child welfare case decisions. A key question for child welfare staff is: *To whom do caseworkers feel most accountable for case planning, their supervisor or a judge?*

As of this writing the National Council of Family Court Judges is working to develop policies for collaborative relationships between child welfare agencies and courts.

Courts have clear roles. However, in making decisions regarding legal rights of the persons involved, legal custody or when youth are in the juvenile justice system, some of whom also may be in foster care.

In the time, several decades earlier, when child welfare more clearly was a social service, court involvement was needed in custody issues, changes of legal status, or when decisions were appealed. Caseloads generally were at least 30, at that time, without overloading staff, and costs were far less than they are now. Caseload standards now are about 15, though there also are variations for different types of cases.

With gradual reduction of professional social work in child welfare with its commensurate "accountability" additions as services deteriorated, it appears that people in positions of influence did not look back and ask what changes contributed to the deterioration. Instead additions were made that, while constructive in concept, accumulated to become a debilitating load for staff, most of whom were not educated for their responsibilities. Throughout this time insufficient attention was given to functions and organizational issues that dealt with needs of caseworkers.

In his book *SYSTEMS THINKING: "You can't just fix one thing*, J. W. Forrester describes what also happened in child welfare. "Our experience in simple terms causes us to look for solutions near the symptoms of trouble; but solving sub-system problems will make other issues worse, and we fail to correct the system problem."

A series of actions all aimed at short-run improvement can eventually burden a system with long-run depressants so severe that even short-run measures no longer suffice. Many current problems are the result of the accumulation of short-run measures taken decades ago.

During the 1950s the educational norm, in at least many states, was that child welfare staff have at least one year of graduate school social work education, with supervisors and administrators having Master's degrees in social work. When that changed, additional accountability measures increased.

As service quality decreased, inadequacies became increasingly apparent. A number of reform efforts were initiated, ranging from legislative strategies and blue ribbon commissions that made recommended changes to improve the systems. When these efforts were not successful, class action litigation was used as a strategy against cities, counties and state child welfare systems, designed to force reform of the systems. In some cases when lawsuits were settled, services were considerably improved. The enormous financial costs and staff time involved have added to the financial burdens of the states and to the over- all cost of child welfare services. There is little data on over-all program improvements for children and their families.

Going back to those simpler arrangements of the past is not possible. But it can be instructional for anyone concerned about program effectiveness, to analyze the basic activities of the agency casework staff needed to carry out the mandate of the laws and the agency's missions. They have to deal with the complexities of the needs of the people they serve and their goals, and the agency goals to help to achieve them. It should not be difficult to consider client needs in the context of the agency's mission and then decide what staff skills and resources are needed to carry out that mission. The purpose of other parts of the organization must enable and assist the casework staff and foster parents, who deal directly with clients, to be effective. This basic organizational principle of planning services from the bottom up has gradually been reduced with mid-level patchwork remedies.

There is only one child in the world. That child's name is "all children."

Will Rogers

Chapter 3

WE ALSO DID IT TO OURSELVES

Or as Pogo said, "We found the enemy and he is us."

The previous chapter focused on changes in child welfare that were imposed from the outside. If those had been the only negative influences, perhaps conditions would be better now than they currently are. But counterproductive changes also were made by people inside the system.

Inherent in child welfare is the fact that many client problems are so complex, sometimes seeming to be intractable, that obtaining a high degree of success is not possible. And for those whose goal is to help people to resolve their problems, this can feel intolerable. Agencies can dealt with that in a variety of ways. It can include trying to improve services, re-defining success, changing definitions or rewriting goals. It also can emphasize organizational issues rather than children's needs, or searching for quick fixes. It can place heavy emphasis on needs of children when they "age out" of care after they spend an inordinate amount of time in foster care, when timely services might have prevented their aging out by becoming a part of a family.

While there are different measures of "success," there is general agreement that it involves permanency planning, i.e. that each child becomes part of a lifetime family, with a minimum of delay. The number of children aging out of the system without family connections is increasing. It rose from 20,000 several years ago to 27,000 at the time of this writing. Of the nearly half million children in care, approximately 19 percent are adopted while 125,000 are awaiting adoption. Although many children are reunified with their birth families, this indicates that large and growing numbers of children are not reunited with their families or adopted.

Some studies indicate that only three percent of young people who have been in foster care go to college and 80 percent of the people in prisons had been in foster care. Currently there is no data to show how many had been connected with families and how many aged out.

A SEARCH FOR PANACEAS

The frustrating reality of limited success contributes to a constant search for panaceas. Legislators and other policy makers, who are not directly involved in providing services, often assume that there is a "silver bullet." Child welfare is too complex for silver bullets, and ideas or theories pushed as major solutions tend to overlook the fact that individualization is a first step in working with children and families. "One-size-fits-all" approaches with novel solutions invariably do violence to some people. Complex issues can seem simple from a distance, but they require complex solutions. Complexity cannot be simplified easily; it has to be dealt with.

When child welfare services were initially carried out by social workers analytical approaches initiated by Sigmund Freud were used extensively. They were useful in helping staff to understand the dynamics of the behavior as well as the attitudes and feelings of persons on their caseloads. This especially included defense mechanisms. However, they gave little practical information about how to use the information excepting with extensive psychoanalysis, which was not feasible in child welfare. It often was assumed that it was applicable to most if not all cases. Resulting disillusionment led to a nearly opposite extreme- "reality therapy." It was hoped that this new approach would be more effective. It wasn't. At one time "treating behavior" (treating symptoms, while ignoring underlying causes) had been considered an insult, but then that approach became acceptable. Only in recent years has Freudianism reemerged in literature as having relevance for understanding children in the system and their families. Their basic needs did not change, but the philosophical basis for dealing with them did.

Many "treatment modalities" came on the scene, often with considerable fanfare. When they do not deliver as promised, they and the originators often quietly fade away. An example of this was "guided group interaction," usually used with groups of teens, especially juvenile delinquents. The approach was basically confrontational, with the group leader, confronting one individual at a time about his or her attitude and behavior. Members of the group were encouraged to participate. A basic assumption was that harmonious relationships do not help youth deal with their problem behavior, but they need to be kept on the defensive through confrontation to face their own behavior. Their feelings were not a priority.

More "modalities" appeared as though each was the new answer, the panacea, such as "operant conditioning" and "transactional analysis." Though they had some value, none were sufficiently applicable to child welfare to serve as the single appropriate approach for every child. Each fad had a new term, or buzz word, which tends to illustrate an adage that buzz words tend to create cottage industries. Many of these ideas might have improved the field, if in the process of implementation, they had been built on what was actually working, instead of being introduced as a completely new, comprehensive approach.

A result of deprofessionalization of child welfare in the 1960s, referred to in the previous chapter, caseworkers lost the ability to make thorough case assessments, thus losing sight of the specific needs of children and families on their caseloads. They then became subservient to the *fad de jour* to guide their case planning. When they lost clarity about individual client's needs, it seemed appropriate to treat everyone the "new" way, assuming that it would be better than previous approaches.

Perhaps, as in all fields, some of the innovations in child welfare are propelled by personal ambition, desire for power and control, competition and also a desire to improve services. Since they may be inherent in human nature, it will not be possible to eliminate them, but the negative effects can be reduced by having new concepts evaluated by persons with various perspectives, rather than simply responding to pressure that sometimes have administrative support.

When judges lost confidence in caseworkers' understanding of the cases and their case plans, many agencies responded by having key people in a case, especially mothers, submit to psychological exams and submit the psychologist's recommendation to the court, as the case plan. This costly process concentrates primarily on one party in the case, without dealing with the full ecology of the child's life. It also tends to put caseworkers further on the sideline, and their "ownership" of cases is further diminished.

This does not suggest that inputs of specialized persons, such as psychiatrists, psychologists and mental health consultants are not valuable. Their involvement can be vital, if used selectively to supplement the caseworker's knowledge in complex cases, rather than replacing the worker's role in assessing cases..

When autism was first recognized as a prevalent and tragic condition for many children, it also was frustrating for people who tried to understand causes and develop treatment techniques. Both were elusive, and in most ways, still are. That gave rise to unusual treatments that would have never been accepted for more normal children. One of these was "aversive therapy," where unresponsive children were treated harshly to try to elicit responses from them. This included harsh slaps on their faces and holding ammonia under their noses, while also holding their mouths shut. Regardless of how sadistic the techniques seemed to be, they were justified as "treatment" by "professional" therapists. When many of the techniques became known, states gradually banned aversive therapy programs, largely through state child welfare licensing programs, since foster children were in many of the programs. Only one state, Massachusetts, did not ban such programs.

State control of punitive programs is not a simple process. It can be easy for them to change terminology, and disguise the activities with different labels, especially under the guise of "treatment" or "education". Parent's desperation, as well as the desperation of child placing agencies responsible for the children, contributed to reluctance of states to ban these programs. Such "helping" programs often charge very high fees.

Boot camps are somewhat similar. When parents and agencies are unable to control teens, sometimes drug addicted, there often are organizations that stand ready to take them. The idea of boot camps took hold quickly and many sprang up. Their appeal apparently was derived from awareness that military boot camps have been a maturing experience for many youth. The extremely successful Civilian Conservation

Corps during the depression gave a positive memory for many people, who expected these boot camps to be similar. Instead many were harsh militaristic, controlling programs that offered few positives, and failed to take into account the fact that many of the youth had serious emotional and behavior problems. After abuse and deaths of a number of youth, boot camps have been banned in many states.

An irony of such programs is that the basic premises may have been sound, but narrow programs and poorly trained staff can turn them into programs very different than those envisioned. The old adage "so near and yet so far" also may apply here. Boot camps in Michigan showed positive results, with no reports of abusive conditions. The fact that Michigan law required that such programs be licensed, and that licensing requirements included basic program components including education, counseling and involvement of families were key factors in providing program quality. Those three program components can make the difference between an abusive and a genuinely therapeutic program.

Wilderness camps in some respects are similar to boot camps. They usually are rather isolated, with heavy program emphasis on control. Some are mobile, making it difficult for state licensing staff to do meaningful licensing. Negative attitudes sometimes develop between staff and children in care, and in circumstances where there is little outside surveillance it should be assumed that abusive conditions will result. A number of deaths also have been reported in wilderness programs.

It can be assumed that most people who chose to work in programs for children and youth are genuinely motivated to help them. Once in the programs however, they see that the work is not as simple as it seemed which can be frustrating and irritating. Some programs fall back on controlling children's behavior rather than understanding individual needs and dealing with them carefully. To complicate it further, the agency treatment approaches sometimes deal less with children's needs than with control and staff convenience. One example of this is "levels" of conformity and privileges in group care that fail to individualize children who may be compelled to conform to what is diametrically opposed to *their* needs. Such dynamics can illustrate a phenomenon expressed by one of Nero's men before he was executed, "Man's greatest inhumanities to man are not done by cruel or evil people. They are done by well-meaning people who are unable to reason from the general to the particular."

State licensing probably provides the single, most effective over-all prevention of abusive conditions in child care and child placement programs, but it is only one of a number of needed safeguards. In several southern states, religiously based agencies had sufficient political influence to be exempted from state licensing. In many instances they were administered by ministers who also had radio programs to raise funds for their programs. Thus the funding source and the source of the children were not in contact with each other and accountability was sharply reduced. Many children, who had been in those programs, reported that extremely abusive conditions existed. Some children even stated that they were required to handle poisonous snakes because snakes would not harm "good" children.

The claim of those program administrators was that they are accountable to God, not the state, and accepting a license is sacrilegious. Ironically, they easily accepted licensure for their cars, school buses, and the airplanes that some of them owned, as well as pilot licenses to operate them. Discussions with these administrators indicated that they especially did not want outsiders to be able to examine agency finances, staff qualifications and discipline practices.

In spite of the protections that state licensing affords, it is not universally accepted. Many states license publicly administered agencies, as well as private, but most do not. Licensing public agencies is more difficult, and enforcement is less clear, relying more heavily on administrative support. Being a police power of the state, licensing has to rely on courts for enforcement. When it involves publicly administered services, especially within the same agency, the process is more complicated. However, holding comparable programs to the same standards, regardless of auspices, is more equitable.

In most states there is at least one licensed agency that has political connections with key legislators or with the governor and is quick to complain if they do not agree with the findings and recommendations of licensing staff, and licensing staff are told to back off. With those agencies, licensing staff are able to do little more than perfunctory licensing studies; if they don't, their jobs are in jeopardy.

An often unrecognized aspect of licensing is that the statutory base makes it possible for licensing staff to look at any part of the program, read any records, and talk with any staff or children, and to report their findings. Licensing enforcement is limited to the state licensing rules, but surveillance to determine what has a bearing on those issues is virtually unlimited. This "openness" factor may be the singular greatest influence of licensing and protection of children in care.

Management by Objectives (MBO), an administrative approach, swept through much of industry in the 1980s and apparently was successful. This approach required staff to establish measurable objectives and plan their work activities accordingly. Since it was considered successful in industry, it was assumed that it also was applicable for child welfare services. In spite of worthwhile basic concepts, it was not a good "fit" for child welfare, where client problems and emergencies are not planned, as work of fire departments cannot be specifically planned in advance. Still this approach burdened child welfare for at least two decades. Top administrators appreciate it because it enables them to see numerically what their staff report. For line staff, it required them to submit reports that served reporting purposes whether or not it reflected the work they actually did or the results. This is another instance of the reality that "the chart is not the patient." Planners and agency administrators sometimes are not aware of what life is like in the "trenches."

Even the Children's Bureau sometimes contributed to confusion. For example it funded many projects to stimulate "collaboration" of child welfare services with other disciplines, especially medical and legal. Unfortunately this occurred after child welfare had lost its self- identity and mission clarity. Meaningful collaboration requires that each entity understands itself to be able to relate effectively with others. These efforts can result in abdication as well as collaboration. Some resulting team efforts were positive, but promoting it, when child welfare service no longer had its own act together, did not help to clarify and reinforce the role of child welfare staff.

Similarly, when it was recognized that positive client outcomes were seriously insufficient, it was assumed that caseworkers were not managing cases well. Even though they might be providing adequate casework, effective management of case activities did not necessarily follow. Then a national effort was made to strengthen case management. Unfortunately, its success caused it to be the major focus in dealing with cases. Casework finally was virtually eliminated, and management became the primary, if not exclusive, approach. As a result, agency staff were called "case managers," and when children or families are recognized as having special needs, such as counseling or other specialized services, agencies often purchase those services, and staff only "manage" them. Thus the caseworker-client relationship was further reduced.

Because Kids Are Worth It!

As stated in the first chapter, much of the thinking in this country shifted from relying on orphanage care for parentless children to substitute family care. However there were limits. Caring for other people's children in groups has a peculiar fascination for some adults.

"Family care" in child welfare generally refers to care by relatives, family foster care or adoption, including adoption by relatives. The majority of children in substitute care are in unrelated family foster homes. These families have been the backbone of child welfare for many decades, but generally they have not been involved effectively as genuine agency team members.

The difference between congregate group care to provide treatment and orphanages sometimes is not easy to distinguish. Historically orphanages tended to be larger, but size is not a distinguishing factor. The purpose of the program is.

Residential group treatment programs are primarily family support services for the child's family, if feasible. If that is not feasible, these programs support another family, such as relatives or adoptive families. Orphanage programs care for children as though the program is an acceptable substitute family, suitable for rearing children. It is all too easy for group treatment programs to hold children longer than is necessary, and in effect provide orphanage-like care, making the distinction even less clear.

Determining whether a group care program works with a clear and united focus can be done with a relatively simple process. This involves two questions asked of a child in care; "Where do you expect to go when you leave here?" and "Approximately when?" The same questions about the child then also are asked of the agency caseworker and a child-care worker. The same process then is done with several other children selected at random. If those people give similar answers for each child, it indicates that case decisions are made by more than one person. It may not clearly reveal the quality of the plan, but it indicates that agency staff work cooperatively toward a goal for each child. If there is no consistency, it indicates that there is no case plan or that people who need to implement it do not know what it is.

When in the Children's Bureau, I occasionally received calls from reporters in communities where orphanages were planned and community resistance had built up. They wanted to hear more about the issues. The conversations were similar. Each time I tried to carefully explain the issues, e.g. that children need families, they need continuity of care when there generally is high staff turnover in group care programs. Children need normal community involvement rather than living in an isolated group. They need to have the hope of developing lifetime family relationships and that with orphanage care they almost inevitably are turned out alone when funding stops, generally at age 18. I also explained that the cost of group care generally is at least 10 times higher than family foster care. In almost every instance, the reporters were not convinced until I asked if their own child, or another child whom they loved, needed a home, would they want that child to grow up in an institution? Invariably, they understood immediately. Apparently they had visualized orphanage care only for "other people's" children.

Occasionally state child welfare agency administrators called, asking which services tend to be better, those administered by public or by private agencies. I replied that both can be excellent or extremely poor services, and the question therefore is not which type is better, but whether they have good leadership. I suggested that both are necessary and recommended that they try to make the ratio as nearly even, or 50-50, as possible. No agency, or group of them, should have a monopoly on children's services and there are benefits for clients to have choices.

Many people in the 1940s to the '60s, were deeply concerned about interracial issues, and believed that integration was the most effective method for dealing with it. In child welfare this resulted in many Afro American children being placed with white foster and adoptive families, supposedly to provide homes that they otherwise would not be able to have. When this continued, the National Association of Black Social workers objected, saying it was a form of racial genocide. Their concerns permeated the field, and a nation-wide taboo against interracial adoption developed. That was in spite of the fact that numerous studies showed positive outcomes for children placed interracially.

At that time I talked with a staff member of a private agency asking if they ever place children interracially. The answer was "no." When asked why not, the reply was "We would like to but the county agency (which pays for services) will not permit it." Knowing staff in the county office, I called there and told about that conversation, wondering what the county policy was, and received an almost identical answer, "We don't mind, but the State Office won't permit it." The next conversation with state office staff was the same, "We don't mind, but the Feds won't permit it." I assured that person that I was a "fed" and there are no prohibitions. Then I asked Elaine Schwartz, the Children's Bureau adoption specialist if there might be something of which I was not aware. She assured me that there were no governmental or national prohibitions. I then called those three people back to clarify that, but do not believe anything changed.

When many frustrated white adoptive applicants complained to their legislators, Senator Metzenbaum of Ohio, in 1994, introduced a bill resulting in the Multi-Ethnic Placement Act (MEPA). It allowed race, color or national origin to be one factor in foster care and adoptive placement decisions, but not the determining factor.

Children's Bureau staff, who were not in sympathy with the law, wrote the regulations for implementing the law as restrictively as possible. When senator Metzenbaum realized what happened, he angrily modified MEPA with the Interethnic Placement Amendments (IEPA) in 1996. It stipulated that race, color or national origin, could not be considered, unless a highly individual assessment determined that these factors should be considered, making it clear that this should be exceedingly rare.

Again because of an extreme position, the pendulum swung to the opposite extreme.

Later when concerned agency staff called asking for advice for dealing with IEPA, I reminded them that they were bound by the law, which is required for their state to be eligible for Federal funds. I also reminded them that the law also states that placements must be "in the child's best interests," and they should hone their creative writing skills to minimize actions damaging to children and reduce the possibility of lawsuits.

"Privatization" which had been promoted in the 1980s suddenly appeared on the child welfare scene in the '90s as the policy that the government supported. The source of this thinking was not clearly identified, but like a fog, it permeated the atmosphere. Forcefully! For some time the boundaries were not clarified. Since most states purchased many services from private agencies, the movement initially seemed redundant. Then it became clear that the intent was for private organizations in states, by contract, to take over and manage the entire child welfare system, acting in place of the state agency. The rhetoric indicated that this could be another panacea which would improve services and lower costs. Unstated in the promotions was the fact that the state agency still would be responsible for monitoring the quality of services provided, thus adding a new bureaucratic layer. Agency accountability to the public is less direct with private agencies than it is with public agencies, since they serve under the authority of governors and state legislators. This also seemed to be overlooked.

In recent years privatization was initiated in a few states, and costs were not reduced or quality increased. Some were recognized as failures and abandoned. Still the "movement" persists.

PERMANCY PLANNING

In the morass of these counterproductive activities, there also was one very bright spot: permanency planning. The concept, developed in the 1960s and '70s was codified in the Adoption Assistance and Child Welfare Act of 1980, PL 96 272. The concepts were not new; most of them had been practiced previously but with this new emphasis the best aspects of practice were "packaged" together as a coordinated way for carrying them out. Demonstration grants were issued to states by the Children's Bureau to implement permanency and a great deal of literature and training was developed to clarify and support the concepts. This reduced the length of time children remained in "limbo" foster care and more of them received lifetime families. The concept is basically simple, that ideally child welfare services result in each child becoming part of a lifetime family. A definition developed in the Children's Bureau is "Permanency planning is the process of helping a child to live in family that offers the hope of establishing lifetime family relationships." An important aspect of this is that when children in foster care become adults and have their own children, those children will have grandparents.

Even though the concepts in permanency planning were not new, the process of getting the field to shift emphasis to apply this basic concept consistently was a major undertaking, requiring huge effort and expense. It may not have happened without the persistent effort of Frank Ferro, the director of the Children's Bureau. The concept that all children need lifetime families and that services must be adapted to carry it out may be the single major contribution to child welfare during the last century, and possibly even this one. Much of the effectiveness of this effort was lost when services quality was reduced, but the concepts and hopefully some materials from that era, as well as relevant new material, will continue to guide child welfare services in the future.

"There is only one child in the world. That child's name is 'all children'."

-Will Rogers

Chapter 4

THE 1980s

Government support and spending priorities vary according to values of Congress and, especially, the president. A playground teeter totter can serve as a metaphor. If the politicians value human services highly, that end of the teeter totter will be high while emphasis on military and law enforcement will be lower. The converse also is true, and that characterized the 1980s. The more conservative the administration, the less it supports human services. The U.S. Children's Bureau, which had been supporting human services since 1912, and was devoted to improving human services, consequently had a difficult time in that decade.

The Children's Bureau and the Child Welfare League of America that it actively cooperated with were the national leaders in the field. They had close working relationships with agencies throughout the country and worked cooperatively to maintain stability during this time.

Two of the significant changes occurring in the 1980s, mentioned earlier, were cancellation of White House Conferences on Children and Youth and an administrative decision to "block grant" funds of Title XX of the Social Security Act.

Congress had allocated $3 million to the Department of Health and Human Services for the Children's Bureau to carry out the White House Conference in 1980, but the new administration directed the Children's Bureau to discontinue work on it and to disseminate the unspent money to the states to develop conferences of their own. There haven't been any subsequent White House conferences on children that had occurred once a decade from 1912 through 1970.

Federal regulations specified that states were required to use a substantial part of Title XX funds to assist parents of children in foster care. With block granting, the money was distributed to states, and they were free to use it for services as they saw fit. The outcome was predictable; in competition with other priorities, children's services generally lose out. Some of the other changes during that decade may have been less significant than these two, but services went consistently "downhill" and the cumulative effect was massive.

A publication division of the Children's Bureau produced a great deal of information about children. Two publications were especially noteworthy: *Your Child from One to Six* and *Children Today*, a semi-monthly publication that included articles about children's issues and services. Those were two

The 1980s

premier national child welfare publications in the country. *Your Child, from One to Six* was a relatively small paperback covered book with information to help parents of young children. It had been published for several decades, and was upgraded every several years. It was reported to be the most read material about young children during the time it was published.

Both these publications were discontinued and the publications division disbanded. The valuable linkage of this division of the Children's Bureau with child-serving organizations and parents was lost. Publication of these, and related materials, were clearly within the statutory mandates of the Children's Bureau that had not been rescinded.

Similarly a research division of the Children's Bureau that helped to stimulate, fund and guide research on children's issues throughout the country also was disbanded.

The bill, signed by President Taft in 1912, established the Children's Bureau with specific mandates, stated previously. The Social Security Act of 1935 further stated that the Children's Bureau "is directed to assist the states through technical assistance, financial aid in enhancing and protecting the well-being of many children for whose health and welfare the States assume responsibility." The Bureau was expected to assist the States with information on the most advanced practices for carrying out these services.

Children's Bureau staff maintained contact with child welfare organizations and personnel throughout the country. This included providing consultation (technical assistance) and training, monitoring research, demonstration and training programs funded by the Children's Bureau, assisting with state and regional conferences and assisting agencies to deal with crises they encountered. Agency personnel from around the country, as well as other countries, frequently visited the Children's Bureau, and also kept in contact through mail, telephone and email when it was developed.

The Children's Bureau specialist staff had expertise in certain aspects of child welfare partly from direct experience in those areas. In the early 1950s there were 53 specialist positions. Agencies used the specialists extensively in planning and refining services. The strong positive difference those staff made was obvious to us in Michigan. Obtaining that role became my personal goal, which I realized 15 years later in 1976, and it lasted for 20 years. But gradually the number of specialist staff positions was reduced, beginning in the 1970s, and government-funded private child welfare resource centers, specializing in specific areas of child welfare service, replaced them. By the end of the century all the Children's Bureau specialist positions had been eliminated.

Effectiveness of specialists in assisting states resulted from a few basic factors. First, they had background experience in, were well informed on subjects they addressed and also became familiar with similar programs in many states. They usually were invited when a need for re-thinking was recognized, sometimes because of a crisis. Their effectiveness also was enhanced by being able to raise innocent-sounding questions in meetings, that staff inside the system wished to ask, but had realistic fear of retribution from high level administrators who were determined to maintain status quo, over which they had control and therefore certain questions were taboo. When issues are brought out in the open, positive change is more likely to occur.

Along with other reductions, government travel funds needed to carry out job responsibilities, was sharply curtailed. Initially the reason given was that travel funds had been reduced. Subsequently it became clear that they had been increased but nearly all the funds were used by politically appointed administrators. When travel that had been considered essential for our responsibilities was cut, I made a number of trips at my own expense, but when our management learned of it, I was told that it could not be permitted. The rationale given was that if one does government work, the government should pay for it, and since the government does not have the funds, it cannot be done. Catch 22 was alive and well.

Staff who were responsible for monitoring projects funded by the Children's Bureau grants were forbidden to visit them. In one instance a staff member in the San Francisco regional office was not permitted to visit a project that was within walking distance from his office. Clearly there was more involved than travel costs.

Having reduced travel time freed up more time for writing. With additional time spent daily in the office and using subway commuting time, I wrote materials that I believed would be helpful to the field. This included many articles. At least 20 were published and dissimilated rather widely.

My role as a specialist in three major areas of child welfare (licensing of children's services, residential group child care and family foster care), formerly was covered by three people. I kept material on hand in each of those areas that I knew would be helpful to people in agencies. In conversations with people around the country at conferences or in telephone calls, I learned their concerns and sent materials to them that they requested or that I believed would be helpful to them. There were few days in the office that I did not mail materials. But then our supply of postage-stamped government envelopes was sharply reduced, and therefore mailing also was reduced. However I noticed that the postage mark on much government mail was photocopied, not embossed or printed. From that time, a photocopied sheet with the postage symbol used as a cover and stapled or taped shut served as well as envelopes. The postage shortage was over.

Those reductions reduced or eliminated some Children's Bureau activity, but the Bureau remained intact and continued to function. Finally, the Bureau itself was threatened. Even though the total number of Federal employees increased during that decade, the administration decided to reduce the number of staff of the Children's Bureau and the larger organization, Human Development Services, together consisting of about 1500 employees. The process for a reduction in force (RIF) was set in motion. Notices were sent to nearly all staff stating that our positions might be eliminated. Several of us, with tacit support of all the other staff, began to work aggressively to stave it off, on our own time and at our own expense. To gain additional support, we joined a federal employees union and received very effective support. Our efforts included, keeping Children's Bureau staff in the ten government regional offices informed about developments, and also sharing information with other child welfare agency personnel throughout the country who valued the Children's Bureau. We contacted and met with legislators, pointing out that available funds could be used to avoid the RIF. They gave strong support. We also confronted the deputy director of our department. The local union representative went on national TV to explain what was happening. But the number of people identified by name for lay-off continued to increase until it reached about 450.

Losing nearly a third of the staff might not have devastated the two organizations, were it not for "bumping" rights. Each person targeted for lay-off had the right to bump another person with less seniority or status. Generally there are at least three bumps for each position eliminated, which would have caused most of the remaining staff to transfer to jobs that they were not prepared for and might not be interested in doing. It was clear then that the life of the Children's Bureau itself was at stake.

The only remaining recourse was to bring a lawsuit against our own department. We collected money from staff and contracted a lawyer, who

Because Kids Are Worth It!

promptly filed a brief in court. A court hearing would have brought the issues into a public arena where the department would have to defend its actions to people it could not control, and would have to accept the court's verdict which also would be public information. The issues also would become a public record. Within three days from the filing, the number of people designated for layoff was reduced to 44. We then stopped our protest activities, those fewer people were laid off, and many staff had to change jobs because of "bumping," but the Children's Bureau remained intact and was able to continue to function.

"The true measure of a nation's standing is how well it attends the children—their health and safety, their material security, their education and socialization, and their sense of being loved and included in the families and countries into which they were born."

UNICEF

Chapter 5

SUPERVISION AND ADMINISTRATION

These subjects include many aspects of agency operations and all have a bearing on the quality and effectiveness of the service. In day-to-day operations this may not be obvious to all agency staff, but each of the components is part of a mosaic that can enhance all the other parts since they are interdependent. Some of them are included here.

SUPERVISION

Most people have someone to whom they are accountable, a supervisor. Only a few of mine seemed to exemplify all the qualities a supervisor should have while some definitely did not. Those between the extremes represented a variety of positions on the continuum. This provided an opportunity to consider many aspects of supervision that affect quality. It also helped me to apply what I learned from it when supervising others.

A major factor determining effectiveness of supervisors is whether they are committed to the mission of the organization, or if their rising in the ranks is paramount to them. However, decisions made by insecure people can be similar to those seeking advancement because they tend to be made for the supervisor's benefit rather than for the mission of the organization. Either of these is difficult for subordinate staff, who sincerely try to prioritize children's and families' needs.

It is reasonable to assume that the supervisor and the supervisee having the same academic background would be an advantage in a supervisory relationship. This is not necessarily true even though it has advantages. Other factors can be at least as significant.

Probably the most significant factor of a supervisor's quality is mental health. In fact good working conditions have been described as "having a mentally healthy supervisor." Obviously, that quality was determined in the past, but it should be considered in hiring or appointing supervisors.

In spite of the different personal qualities supervisors bring to the role, there are several qualities of good supervision that anyone can try to incorporate. The supervisor:

- takes responsibility for knowing agency policies and its resources
- clarifies expectations of staff performance

Supervision and Administration

- maintains positive relationships with other units of the agency where cooperation is needed
- works to keep communication open with top administrators, as well as downward. The latter takes more effort because it is more difficult
- accepts that their role is to educate, support, guide, encourage and when necessary, control subordinates
- encourages each staff member to do quality work and is supportive of their efforts.
- promotes team effort among subordinate staff
- listens to staff concerns, recognizing that they may be about either job activities or their feelings about them
- is comfortable with the fact that some subordinates know more about some things than s/he does, without feeling threatened. There is a tendency to assume that the person with the most rank also knows the most; this may be true of certain things, but not everything. The more comfortable both parties are with this, the more effective they can be
- is sensitive to special needs of staff, including discouragement and burnout
- corrects staff when necessary
- has a sense of humor

When selecting staff, administrators and supervisors sometimes select those with limited ability, so that they will not be a threat to them, rather than attempting to select the highest quality persons available. The irony of this is that they quickly become known and judged by the quality of the work of the people they supervise. This has been described as being head pipsqueak if one selects "pipsqueaks", or as head tiger if one selects tigers. In my experience, brighter staff are much easier to supervise. The standing that supervisors have in their agency is largely determined by the performance of the staff they supervise; therefore they have a vested interest in helping them to perform effectively.

Some personnel in leadership positions believe that their security is primarily in their relationship with their own supervisor, and are not as concerned about loyalty of the staff they supervise. Actually the opposite can be true. Relationships with just one supervising person can change unexpectedly, for a variety of reasons, leaving that person without a support base. When the team of the staff one supervises feels team unity and productivity, with good leadership, their loyalty generally is stronger and is a more dependable support base than a relationship with one supervisor. Effective supervisors invest in developing strong working relationships with people they supervise. High quality of their work can provide job security for the supervisor.

Line staff are aware that even in an agency with rather poor management but with a strong supportive supervisor, they can accomplish a great deal. Conversely even in a good agency, staff who experience "problem" supervision find it difficult to work effectively or to feel good about their jobs.

When a supervisor unfairly harasses a staff member in the working group, there is a tendency of others in the group to avoid the victim, to avoid displeasing the supervisor. They also may be relieved that someone else is being picked on, rather than they. This only feeds the problem, because they too may in turn become the *victim de jour*. To maintain peer unity, staff not being subjected to harassment will rally around that "victim," being as openly supportive as possible. Thus, the feeling of isolation intended for the staff member instead becomes the supervisor's. There *is* strength in unity.

What advice can be given to someone being unfairly harassed? First, do the job you were assigned, as well as possible. Second, maintain positive working relationships with co-workers. Third, network with others in the agency, and the community, as appropriate, to keep lines of communication open with others who have influence. Fourth, consider carefully whether the matter should be escalated to higher administrative levels, and if so, how. Fifth, don't panic, but try to be patient; sometimes unexpected administrative changes occur that resolve the problem.

ADMINISTRATIVE ISSUES

There are many ways to categorize personnel attitudes. One of them is the question of whether they came to the job because of a strong interest in the program of the agency and a desire to make a positive difference. Some come to the agency simply because a job is available and may offer career advancement potential. While there is no clear-cut distinction between these attitudes, it is a factor that can determine the way they make decisions.

When an agency undergoes a major change or is under stress, staff who are committed to providing services are the most troubled because their work opportunities are thwarted. They then may be inclined to leave the agency. Not being able to be productive matters less to staff who are not committed to service but are more concerned about their position in the chain of command, and they keep looking for opportunities for advancement. When the turmoil has passed, as it eventually does, many service-oriented people have left, while those remaining are even more in control. Service-oriented staff need to understand that in a career with a large agency there may be periods when they cannot do much more than tread water, but it is a price that may have to be paid to help maintain agency quality and their continued career growth.

There is an administrative adage that "organizational interests come first." Clearly agency security and survival are essential, but only if the emphasis does not override the agency purpose for existence. Both are needed and keeping a healthy balance can be difficult. Agencies have many ways of protecting themselves, some healthy, some less so. Positive methods include providing quality services based on needs, with openness throughout the system and to the public. Richard Cloward, a sociologist, said that "The system is what people say it is." This can be unfortunate because organizations can place more emphasis on projecting a positive public image than

Supervision and Administration

on providing quality services. Members of foster care review boards recognize the difference between the image of an agency and the quality of its services.

My observations when licensing agencies were surprising in this regard. Some agency directors believe that their program is excellent. Other directors readily admit that their program has weaknesses and flaws. Thorough licensing studies tend to reveal the opposite. Because of the complexity and changes that occur in every agency, perfection can never be realized. Agency directors who perceive their programs as flawless are not adequately familiar with their own program, and probably are not familiar with new developments in the field. If they believe their program is "the best" there is no need to try to improve. Directors who do not claim perfection are aware of flaws in their system and constantly work to improve the program. As a result their programs tend to be of higher quality. What is a definition of a good agency? "One that always tries to improve" has been suggested.

Agencies of nearly any size often have two types of administrators, the director and a person second in command, or who also may be responsible for a segment of the program. If the director is a stern person who is not easily approachable, the other person generally will be a pleasant, well informed, caring professional person, who can represent the agency positively to people who are interested in knowing whether the agency will provide quality services. Agency staff also appreciate those persons. Conversely, if the agency director is approachable and represents quality service, there often is a "hatchet man" to keep staff within the agency in line, or to "keep their feet to the fire." Sometimes the "hatchet man" is the defacto administrator of the agency. Either arrangement can provide a "good cop, bad cop" arrangement. Any agency administrator would be well advised to wonder if that phenomenon is operating and how it affects the services provided by the agency

When an agency, or a component of a large agency, has genuine high quality, it often is perceived by others as simply being a good organization or a part of one. That overlooks the fact that quality did not develop spontaneously. There was a visionary person, a "spark plug", who was able to conceptualize the program, articulate it to people who needed to understand it, provided inspiration and worked very, very hard to get it implemented and operating.

Obviously the administrator or board to whom that person was responsible also gave the "spark plug" freedom to carry it out. If that person is able to select and guide staff for the program, the quality may continue after s/he has left if the vision, understanding and commitment were clearly understood. Administering a quality program may look easy, but it too requires a great deal of work. Ruth Bowen, an excellent director of the Child Welfare Division of the Michigan Department of Public Welfare in the 1950s and 60s, had a cartoon on her office wall, showing a duck on a calm pond, with a caption, "A duck may look calm on the surface, but he is paddling like hell underneath."

In my role as administrator of Michigan child welfare licensing and later in the U.S. Children's Bureau, there were many opportunities to see this distinctive type of leadership operating.

A phenomenon that may not be readily apparent is that status quo is a very powerful "force," no matter how good or bad an agency is. Vested interests and personal security of administrative staff can be virtually impervious to change. "Good", for example, can be perceived as a lack of negative publicity. When serious problems, including tragedies, occur in a large agency, such as a state department, and it receives public and political attention, corrective action is initiated. This often includes one of the following:

1. a study is conducted
2. a consultant is brought in
3. some high-level staff are fired
4. the agency is reorganized
5. a combination of the above

The irony is that these responses can take up to two years, with initial expectation of constructive changes, but after two years public and legislative interest has shifted, and the agency may be able to continue with little or no change.

When agencies are started, or new services are added, it normally involves careful study and planning, including cost analysis, to develop a level of service quality. However, when there is budget shortfall and retrenchment is needed "across the board," reductions frequently are made, with funds for each program component reduced by a small percentage. The federal government uses the term "sequestering" for this approach. Unfortunately this reduces quality in all services of the organization. Eliminating one program component entirely protects other services, and the result of the budget reduction then is unmistakably clear, and could lead to efforts to restore that program component.

When agencies are first established, the purpose of the services guides planning, with assessment of needs of the staff and foster parents, who provide direct service to clients. Planning then is done from the bottom up. Later when changes are necessary, adjustments at various levels of the organization are made, often with less regard for the needs of personnel who provide direct services. That consideration is as basic then as it is in initial planning.

RESPONSE TO NEGATIVE PUBLICITY

In the mid '70s, tragedies in child welfare services in a large county in Michigan received negative public attention. That led to an internal study by competent agency staff, taking about six months. They conducted a thorough, detailed study and issued an excellent report, except for one thing. The chairman of the study committee said they encountered a surprising phenomenon. Within the morass of problematic agency services, they found a few units that were exemplary. Staff worked well together and moral was high. Interviews with staff indicated that they were well-informed and worked with clear focus. Case records also revealed quality work with positive outcomes. However, in each of those instances the supervisor or low level administrator responsible for that unit was perceived as a maverick and was not in the good graces of the agency. Those administrators emphasized client needs more than organizational interests, so they were not appreciated. One would have hoped that the study report would have included this observation, with a recommendation that the agency examine the work of these units to determine whether their procedures could be implemented agency-wide. As of this writing the entire state agency is struggling to settle a class action lawsuit, based primarily on severe problems in the county where this occurred.

Until the 1950s, state agency directors were the only persons in the organizations who were appointed by governors. They could be removed for cause, but generally continued for extended periods even with the change of governors and political affiliation. In addition, they had an active three member advisory board, also appointed by the governor. Thus, while they were accountable to the governor and legislators, they often could more comfortably respond to client needs because they had some support from influential people who were more likely to understand the issues. Then that changed. President Carter signed legislation, making it possible for additional administrative staff in the federal system to be appointed politically and some were. Then President Reagan used that change to mandate that additional layers of staff were politically appointed. Generally, now only persons politically appointed can make policy decisions. States followed suit and also have multiple layers of appointed high-level staff.

Occasionally political appointees have a background in programs they administered, but the common denominator in their appointments and performance requirements is political loyalty. With political party shifts, something akin to an earthquake can go through the agency system. Among many ramifications of this, two unexpected ones sometimes emerge. A positive one was that it often breaks up fiefdoms. Some administrators over time seem to feel that they own the units they are responsible for and trying to collaborate with them can be difficult unless they see a clear self-interest. Shifts in administrative control sometimes improve that aspect of the work environment. A negative side, however, is that some staff who seemed to embrace certain values rather quickly adapt to very different values. When a change of political party in power occurs, some of them seem to quickly embrace very different values.

USES OF POWER

There are two major types of non-physical power-force and influence. Force can take many forms and is exercised most often in administrative authority through orders given to subordinates. Force may or not have substance, but it is expected to get results quickly. There are many circumstances in which it is essential, such as military combat, some kinds of law enforcement, and during surgery. Then a high degree of control is essential. However, an organization's authority often is perceived as evidence of success and consequently is a goal for many. People who use force appear to be strong but sometimes actually are insecure, and using force seems to project strength. When they are confronted with equal or greater force, they often appear weak. When they leave the agency, they tend to be forgotten quickly because they, or their name, did not convey substance that is valued. Any administrator should keep in mind Lord Akton's observation that "Power tends to corrupt...."

The difference between authoritarianism and authoritative administration may not be readily obvious, but fundamentally they are virtual opposites. Authoritarianism is the exercise of power for its own sake, often demanding unquestioned obedience. In contrast, authoritative leaders also exercise power given to them legitimately but use it in a way that gives priority to carrying out the mission of the organization.

Influence, as opposed to force, can be exercised by people with or without authority. It requires knowledge of the subject and ability to persuade and involves a certain amount of teaching, mutual respect and understanding. When staff carry out what they learn from influence, they incorporate it into their own values that tend to be lasting.

When people obtain positions of authority, they and others tend to assume that they know enough to be able to make knowledgeable decisions about the area for which they responsible. That is never fully possible. Shared decision making almost always is more effective. When complex decisions are needed, supervisors or administrators on almost any level make sounder decisions when they are discussed with subordinate staff, and sometimes others. Each person may see aspects of the issue that others do not see.

Bringing issues out in the open makes it easier for the administrator to make well-informed decisions. Perhaps equally significant, when staff have an opportunity to discuss an issue before a decision is made they develop a sense of ownership and will be more inclined to support it enthusiastically. While this is shared decision-making the decisions are not group decisions. Once the decision is made, the person in charge is fully responsible for it, but that process for arriving at decisions can raise morale, enthusiasm and loyalty. This process for making administrative decisions can be deceptively simple, but it is characteristic of authoritative leadership and can be a major factor affecting staff loyalty, cooperation and performance.

"We trained hard, but it seemed that every time we were beginning to form up teams we would be reorganized. I was to learn late in life that we tend to meet any new situation by reorganizing, and a wonderful method it can be for creating the illusion of progress while producing confusion, inefficiency, and demoralization."

PETRONIOUS ARBITER
210 B.C.

Chapter 6

SEMANTICS

Words are powerful. They carry meaning from one person to another or from one person to many in a speech or in writing, at a certain time or even centuries later. That may be obvious, but the benefits of careful articulation may not be as obvious. One of the great masters of language and expressing concepts was Shakespeare, but there are five times as many words in the English language now as there were when Shakespeare lived. That suggests that there is much more potential for expressing ideas, but also more potential for error and unnecessary complexity.

When one considers the importance of clear semantics in the context of the needs of children in the child welfare system, it is clear that careful communication is of extraordinary importance. That does not require fastidious attention to "in" terminology, or esoteric language, but rather that it be free from ambiguity and redundancy. Unnecessary words also detract from clarity. Simplicity, if sufficient to cover the subject, usually is the most clear.

In spite of the incredible importance of child welfare services and the corresponding need for clear understanding, it is a field with a surprising amount of loose terminology. This is an attempt to clarify some of that terminology, with the assumption that it can help to improve child welfare services.

When we communicate, we hope that the meaning each person expresses is clear to the other, although it is possible for us to talk past each other without realizing it. That constitutes a waste of effort and more seriously, the possibility that misdirected activity will result. Using clear terminology at least reduces that possibility.

Some examples of unclear terms sometimes used in child welfare are:

Foster care. *Foster care* is a generic term. It refers to either family care or group care. When it is necessary to distinguish them, it can be done simply with the term, *family foster car* or *group foster care*.

Placement and **care.** These terms convey entirely different meanings and require clear distinctions. The original meaning of placement was "placing out," (i.e. children being placed away from their families). Thus they are not subsequently placed with their families, but may be *returned* to them, or *reunited* with them.

Sometimes the term *"placement"* is used to denote a child, foster home, an opening in a foster home or a status, as a child is "in placement." All these are inaccurate. A grammatically correct statement would be, "After the child was removed from her home, she was *placed* into *care* in a foster home"...or *"placed into a foster home."* Placement is an act, a verb, referring to the activity of selecting a foster home and bringing the child to it. Once there, the child is in *care*.

Assure and **ensure.** Child welfare literature and conversations both are liberally sprinkled with these terms. Often they are intended to claim that certain activities will result in a particular outcome. These terms are tantamount to "guarantees" and there is virtually no such thing in child welfare. It is not difficult to make a more accurate statement, e.g., "If the caseworker sees the child regularly, it is *more likely* that the case plan will be carried out," rather than "...assures that the case plan will be carried out." It is clearer and more accurate.

When writing and conversation is laced with those terms, it implies that desired results will occur and that they are possible, even when they may not be. It might be better if those terms were completely removed from child welfare language, with one exception. When one party is required to hold a second party responsible for certain activities, the term may be applicable, (e.g. "The agency must *insure* that all drivers have a valid driver's license.") It cannot claim that drivers having licenses will insure safety.

Casework and **case management.** For many years, the term *"caseworker"* was used to refer to line child welfare staff. This assumed that when children on their caseload needed casework service, they provided it. Nearly all line staff once had at least partial social work graduate school training, so their providing casework was feasible, within their time limitations. In unusual instances where case complexity exceeded their skill, they obtained specialized services from other specialists. With reduction of social work education for most child welfare staff, for many years only a fourth of them had any social work training, the professional skill level dropped sharply. In addition, the *"accountability"* activities mentioned previously also reduced the amount of time they had available for each client. Increasingly, caseworkers were unable to provide direct services and also manage the case activities well. Then, in part from federal leadership, state agencies were encouraged to place high priority on managing cases, rather than providing services themselves.

The Children's Bureau issued many grants to states to help them to develop improved case management skills. But that effort did not address the need to balance casework and management, and the value of casework was further diminished. That also gave the erroneous impression that one person can understand the complex needs of their clients and be able to arrange for specialized services to meet those needs. Social work professionalization also was deemphasized, and some jurisdictions found it easier to reduce staff salaries because of the assumption that professional social work skills were not required.

The term *case manager* was then used for line staff, and when a child or parent needed special services, they obtained the service, such as psychological testing, drug treatment or counseling services, at considerable additional expense. The term *"wrap-around service"* was used to describe the process of obtaining needed services for clients, but few if any of them were provided by agency staff. The term *case manager* contributed to this diminished role of agency casework staff.

This worker. At one time staff providing services in public assistance referred to themselves as "visitor" in case reports. That depersonalized reporting served no useful purpose but made case record reporting awkward. At that time such use of labels was not done in child welfare, but first person pronouns were used, making reporting easier and clearer, without having to use contorted language to make a simple statement. The stock-in-trade, or essence, of child welfare is relationships and plain English made it easier to report activities and conversations with clients.

It was with considerable concern that in recent years I learned that, at least in many states, caseworkers refer to themselves as *this worker* in reporting their activities in the case record. This use of a label, a mask, tends to depersonalize activities and relationships. It often seemed as though identity of the worker was not clear. Questions asked of many administrators about this did not produce any reasons for it. Line staff had various opinions, but a few said they felt more comfortable with the term because with it they did not feel as exposed. A question is whether the record should clearly reflect a staff member's participation in the case activities or disguise it.

Foster child. Children in foster care are foster children, aren't they? No they are not. *Foster child* is a label, which seems to place all such children in the same category, as though they are similar, and different than other children. They all are individual children, as are other children, and need to be thought of as individuals in their own right.

There is a caveat here. There are occasional times when avoiding the terms *foster child* or *foster children* requires awkward wording. The practical thing to do then is to go ahead and use them for those instances, but only then. All children need to know that we see them as individuals, not a part of an inferior category of people. Sometimes we also need to be reminded. Our terminology should indicate respect for them individually wherever possible.

Permanency planning. Concepts in permanency planning were not new when it was developed in the 1960 and '70s. Rather it took concepts and practices that had been understood and used successfully and assembled them together into a coherent package. It became a centerpiece or core value of child welfare. The meaning is very simple. Children need lifetime families, and the goal of services is to make that possible. A Children's

Bureau definition was that it is the process of helping a child to live in a home that offers the hope of establishing a lifetime family relationship. The definition does not designate any particular category of family.

It has not been possible for agencies to achieve this goal for a high percentage of children for whom they are responsible. Various programs have been developed for children who left the system without family connections, including independent living services. The need for clarity between permanency planning services and services provided to children as they "age out" is significant because the activities and goals in permanency planning and aging out services are different, being almost diametrically opposed. Permanency planning normally is "Plan A" initially for all children in the system, and when that is not successful, Plan B is needed. This does not suggest that aging out services are not valuable, but that they are different and are applied when the preferred goal cannot be reached. It is too easy to broaden the meaning of permanency planning, implying that agency successes in achieving permanence are greater than they actually are.

Some agency records also indicate a lack of clarity between permanence and stability in care. Stability in care is invaluable, and may be conducive to permanency planning, but does not in itself provide lifetime families.

A practical question that can quickly clarify the difference between permanency planning and other services is "Which service is likely to result in the children of the children now in the system to have grandparents?"

Independent living. This term which represents many kinds of valuable services is a misnomer. Normal living is interdependent living, not independent living. That term implies isolation. Other terms such as "self-sufficiency" may have been more accurate, but "independent living" is so firmly established and now represents an array of valuable services, that attempting to change it would be confusing. However it is important for agency staff to be clear about the need for all young people to develop skills and to become interdependent.

Rules and regulations. These terms mean the same thing. Using them both not only is redundant, but can be confusing to persons who are not aware of that, and may assume that they represent different things and being familiar with both might be necessary.

Many terms come and go, each trying to make an impact on the system, such as "customer" instead of client, and "stake holder' referring to other involved organizations. Such novel terminology may seem to suggest an elevated level of sophistication, but rarely adds clarity. However it is likely that new terms will keep sprouting up. Some may even help.

There are times when using esoteric language, especially among fellow professionals, can express ideas more efficiently and clearly. Generally, however using plain English is more likely to improve understanding and communication between people. With most conversations, using precise language is not essential, because both parties usually arrive at an understanding. Written material usually also can convey meaning well enough to have the desired effect. What is not true of most speaking or some writing, however, is that it affects the well-being of a third party, in this case large numbers of children. When the content relates to services for those children, clarity takes on great importance.

It is common for children in foster care to be referred to as "vulnerable." While that is true, it inadequately expresses their circumstances. All of us are vulnerable, whereas most of these children are literally helpless. That suggests that we need to be exceptionally careful to clearly and accurately convey what we mean because their circumstances often are precarious, and our clarity is their right.

There also are circumstances when customary terms and generalizations do not fit particular situations well and exceptions fit the circumstances better. This can be helpful if it also is recognized that they are exceptions and do not become precedent-setting. Winston Churchill, whose masterful use of the English language was widely recognized, made that point when he was criticized for ending a sentence with a preposition, violating a recognized grammatical principle. He replied that such "narrow consistency is errant pedantry, up with which I cannot put."

"Words, like glasses, obscure everything they do not make clear."

Joseph Joubert

Chapter 7

REBUILDING

People familiar with current child welfare services know that improvements are needed. Opinions about what is needed vary tremendously and change over time. Many of us can suggest remedies, but no one sees the whole picture, or sees it from the perspective of each of the people in his or her various roles. Line staff probably see the inadequacies most clearly, while people at higher administrative levels see the big picture more clearly. People outside the system are aware of tragedies that are made public, but rarely understand what is needed to operate services well.

This chapter is an attempt to show changes that can improve child welfare services from the perspective of a person who had many vantage points, direct casework, statewide and nationwide responsibility, and from conversations with thousands of people in virtually every role in child welfare in every state, as well as child welfare personnel in several countries. There is no assurance that they are fully accurate and certainly are not complete, but they include collective knowledge and perspective of many people and seem worth sharing.

Of all the changes needed, two seem primary, in that while many are important, none of them will operate effectively if these two do not also occur. They are increased social work training for child welfare agency staff, and getting the heavy bureaucratic burdens off the workers, freeing them to do the jobs for which they are responsible.

TRAINING

Other professions, such as law, engineering, medicine, nursing and teaching, have an academic, professional base. They would quickly lose their basic knowledge and effectiveness without those foundations. Social workers in child welfare once had such a foundation, but it was lost in most states. Several studies have shown that social work training improves child welfare case outcomes, worker satisfactions and improved tenure. That investment reduces costs and improves outcomes for children and their families who are in the system.

But how? The effort begins with recognition that we must put child welfare back into social work and social work into child welfare. Child welfare content has been removed from social work curriculums in many colleges and universities which do not adequately prepare students for that specialty. Such content is needed not only in curriculums, but university faculty who specialize in child welfare can also teach it to agency staff in adult education. With CEUs, now needed for social work licensure, agencies have a strong vested interest in helping to implement this. How can universities develop faculty skills for this? Part of the answer is relatively simple—select faculties who have had successful child welfare practice experience. Recognizing that there are times when this is more valuable than doctoral degrees is not professional heresy.

One of the trends in social work education is increasing the number of part-time adjunct faculty by selecting professional practitioners to teach some (or even many) child welfare practice courses. This is practical, less costly than full-time tenured faculty, and generates a larger variety of course offerings. Tenured faculty also can work part time in agencies or in other cooperative efforts with agency staff.

Agencies and universities having a continual feed-back helps them to keep the needs of agency practice constantly flowing into the academic base and then back into practice through graduating students. One method to promote this dialog is to create faculty-worker exchange programs in which the university faculty and agency practitioners exchange roles for a time, such as a semester. The benefits of this are enormous. The object is to immerse the faculty members in current agency practice, needs, policy and culture while also enriching school courses with practitioner's knowledge and skills for students interested in child welfare.

Neither agencies nor universities operate effectively in a vacuum. They need each other, but there also are two other major national players, the

National Association of Social Workers (NASW) and the Council on Social Work Education, (CSWE.) NASW has shown rather little active interest in child welfare in the past, but this essential ingredient may now be improving. Probably most school of social work faculty are aware of the role or CSWE because it establishes educational standards. Agency staff may be less aware of this, even though they are indirectly affected by it. In the past CSWE encouraged generic teaching of social work with little specificity for specialized areas of social work practice. This did not adequately serve the interests of students who chose specialties like child welfare. Generic training may have somewhat more relevance for bachelor's programs, but many students who intend to take child welfare positions can benefit from knowing what they will encounter when they have responsibility for cases. Inter-organizational communication among these four entities is essential for achieving a relevant nationwide educational system that prepares students for service in child welfare.

This may seem relatively clear, until one considers the fact that each state has a number of schools of social work, both graduate and undergraduate as well as public and private, and some are inclined to operate rather independently. This indicates a need for coordination of efforts. Having at least one person in each state provide statewide coordination and leadership to increase coordinated effort can improve the program of each school.

The parts of the machine needed to make child welfare run effectively often are not apparent to people in the other parts of the system. Extra effort by leaders in each part to network together can help people throughout the systems to see their own efforts become more effective and also enhance other aspects of the system, improving services to children and their families.

Adequate training also affects staff tenure and reduces agency costs. The expense of hiring a new caseworker is comparable to half to three-quarters of an annual salary of one staff member. Staff who understand what they are doing and are recognized for it tend to remain.

Most training of foster parents is done by the child-placing agencies that use them. Their training can be as important as casework staff training, since they have most direct involvement with children and often also are in touch with their parents. Their training directly affects the way the mission of the agency is carried out. Much of the training can be done by state and local associations of foster parents, but normally they do not have reliable funding sources, and need agency assistance to cover some of the costs. Local associations of foster parents provide an identity for foster parents in an area that relationships with their agencies cannot provide.

Some training for casework staff also is appropriate for foster parents. Arranging it as joint effort has many benefits for both. Because the casework role in working with foster parents has aspects of supervision, supervisory training for those staff also is beneficial. Retention of foster homes is greater when staff carry out their roles sensitively and skillfully.

Role-related training for all the personnel in the system needs to be considered in planning for training. This includes administrators, secretaries, judges and lawyers.

Various studies show that casework staff tenure affects many aspects of performance in child welfare. A recent study in Milwaukee showed that if a child has only one caseworker, the likelihood of that child achieving permanence is 70 percent. With two caseworkers it drops to 17 percent, and with three workers it drops to 3 percent. Clearly staff retention is critically significant.

Even good things come with price tags. A potential negative resulting from training is the personal status and prerogatives that it can provide. Though good in themselves, they can create a hierarchy of status that is intimidating for some people without the same background, especially foster parents, reducing needed communication and mutual respect. Much of the knowledge about children's feelings and behavior is known by non-degreed people, especially foster parents. Practical first-hand knowledge can be as valuable as professional judgment. Both perspectives, practical and theoretical, are needed. The thinking that goes into case planning and decisions always must contain common sense. None of the involved parties has a corner on that market.

ENABLING STAFF TO DO WHAT THEY NEED TO DO.

The burdens on agency casework staff include paperwork, the accumulation of monitors and accountability measures mentioned in the second chapter. They include foster care review boards, court appointed special advocates (CASAs), state and federal audits, guardians ad litem (GARs), judges who, sometimes providing virtual supervision beyond protection of client rights and press scrutiny when problems are made public. Often after serious service performance flaws are identified, an additional monitoring process is implemented or additional reporting is required. For normal casework activities, a worker's feeling that s/he is accountable to more than one person is counterproductive. Studies indicate that workers report that from 50 to 75 percent of their time is spent on paperwork. The tragic irony of this is that client-staff relationships are the essence of child welfare but staff have little time to spend with children.

These monitoring measures were set up incrementally over a long period of time, as service inadequacies became exposed. Reassessing them in a unified process that examines what can be reduced or discarded is needed now. Each state might need its own way of dealing with this since some of the accountability procedures and reporting requirements are state-specific.

Many other improvements are within reach of state agencies, but unless the issues of workers heavy reporting requirements as well as adequate education and training occur, effectiveness of other changes will be limited. Expertise and sufficient time to implement it are basic to carrying out the complex responsibilities of caseworkers.

CASE ASSESSEMENTS

One of the most essential skills of a child welfare worker is making good case assessments. But that skill gradually diminished with deprofessionalization. A case assessment is the foundation on which a case, or service plan, is built.

As stated previously, the issues or needs that brought the client-families to the agency contain both presenting problems and underlying problems. Presenting problems generally are tangible, such as lack of resources, lack of parents' willingness or ability to care for children, inadequate housing, death or other absence of a parent or abusive behavior. Underlying causes are more subtle, with longer roots, often intergenerational, having to do with family relationships, sometimes including abusive, harsh or neglectful child rearing, unemployment, poverty, chronic alcohol or drug addiction.

While dealing with presenting problems usually is needed immediately, that may not affect long-range family problems or conflicts that will reemerge if not dealt with. Professional case assessment is needed to understand both presenting and underlying problems if the agency is to give effective immediate assistance and also develop a case plan for helping the family achieve long-range stability.

Rebuilding

The major reason for assessing cases is to understand if there are sufficient positives in a family to make it worth involving them in a child's life and how to help them to come to grips with counterproductive behavior. This assessment is not a risk assessment, which is done prior to making a decision of whether to remove a child. If a risk assessment reveals such destructive relationships or dangerous conditions that continued care of the child cannot be considered, then some aspects of a case assessment would not be relevant. However, medical history always is valuable for understanding children's future needs. Learning about relatives, including siblings, who may be supportive, also is useful. Frequently there are more strengths in a family than are apparent during emergencies and hasty negative assumptions should be avoided.

Casework or counseling can help children connect their past with their current feelings and circumstances, in the context of planning toward the future. Information obtained about underlying causes can help to make this possible. Children almost universally blame themselves for the family breakup though this usually is not the case. Their having some understanding of cause and effect regarding their family's disintegration can help them to move on with their lives.

So what should be included in a case assessment? The following list is not exhaustive, but contains many of the basics, and assumes that it is done by social work staff. The list does not specify methods or timing; however, assessments always are subject to change as new information or circumstances become known.

1. <u>Physical and dental exams for children AND the mother.</u> This helps todetermine which "causes" may have a physical origin and need to be dealt with independently.

2. <u>Identification of presenting problems.</u> These usually are the reasons that brought the family to the attention of the agency, and deeply concern the family, or someone who feels responsible for the child.

3. <u>A social history.</u> Some problems of the family are of recent origin, e.g. death of a parent, divorce, an accident, home foreclosure, job loss or drug use. A social history can reveal the level of the family functioning prior to the current critical conditions. Learning about the family's history two or three generations earlier, if possible, may reveal a pattern of the difficulties that gave rise to the current problem. Information about parents' work history, previous residences and family connections are useful. Understanding those factors will help to reveal both the strengths and weaknesses of the family, hopefully enabling the agency to identify strengths to build on.

4. <u>A record of the child's immunizations, if available.</u>

Rebuilding

5. <u>A description, possibly including a genogram or echogram, showing all the persons who are important to the child and family, especially those who have been supportive</u>. Listing all the members of the immediate family as well as extended family members, with their location, and evidence of positive or negative influence on the family may identify valuable resources. List special needs of the family, such as day care or drug treatment. Identify siblings and their current location and status.

6. <u>Identify goal of the parents and their children</u> to determine whether the agency can realistically support them.

7. Determine, after a RISK assessment was done, if it is realistic for the child to remain home, or be returned, and whether special services are needed. If the child is removed, recommend the type of substitute care needed, (e.g. family foster care or residential treatment, and what kind). When feasible, identify programs that are equipped to meet those needs. Include at least preliminary recommendations for permanency planning i.e. the type of lifetime family connection that seems feasible.

A case assessment report is a discrete document.

If family conference planning is used, the need for information about extended family members may be reduced because some of those people will be able to directly clarify their potential for support.

It may not be possible for a caseworker to accomplish all this quickly, but it can be useful as a check list to obtain as much of the information as possible, before making a case plan.

Many children enter the system through emergency shelter care, which may last for a day or a few weeks, and in extreme cases, even months. This is an opportune time to collect social history and other information about the family. With group shelter care the shelter care staff, in collaboration with the caseworker, are in the best position to obtain this information. If the child is in a family emergency shelter care home, the caseworker is in the best position to carry this out, with inputs from the foster parents. With this basic information, it should be possible to for an agency to develop realistic case plans toward permanence for the child, with all involved parties working in concert toward that goal. It also reduces potential for unnecessary subsequent moves for the child. Assessments may need to be revised as circumstances change, with case plans also adjusted to fit.

COMMUNICATION

Good communication doesn't in itself make positive changes, but without it efficiency is impossible. Only a few suggestions and principles are given here. Perhaps the most fundamental ingredients

Rebuilding

in communication are clarity and honesty. Internal agency communication, as well as communication with persons outside the agency, sometimes is sprinkled with defensive, less than fully disclosed information, or exaggerated accomplishments. Even when case decisions are made, presumably "in the child's best interests" the question of whether it is genuinely in the child's interest or for staff convenience must be considered. Honesty may be the single most important cross-cutting issue in operating child welfare as an effective service, and self-monitoring by each person on what they say or write can contribute to the quality of the service..

Agency staff sometimes feel that they cannot afford to be honest, but there is at least one time when it can be safe as well as productive. When they leave their organization and feel that systemic factors detracted from their performing effectively, a memo or letter to multiple layers of administrators could provide valuable information to those administrators who otherwise would not be aware of circumstances and needs in the programs they administer.

Information flows in all directions, and attempts to keep it accurate and useful are a major organizational need. Downward information generally receives the most attention, but care is needed to be sure that it is understood at the lower levels. It often requires accompanying training. Moving information upward often is more difficult and also more lacking. Unless top-level administrators know how their policies are playing out on the worker level, they don't know how well the mission of the agency is being carried out. It is reported that Napoleon was not as brilliant a strategist as he was given credit for. Often in evenings when the sun went down and war stopped, most generals talked together in their tents. Then, he met with troops at the front to learn what they were encountering and what they needed, and then was able to make more effective decisions. That process also can benefit child welfare.

Child welfare agencies operate within a large array of other organizations that also impact children and families. If staff are encouraged to communicate with them, everyone benefits. This may develop spontaneously with mutual interest in cases, but specific staff assignments for this also are beneficial.

Agency directors frequently are confronted by news media, at times when they least want it, i.e. when tragedies occur or serious mistakes become known. The content of these episodes can be easier to handle if the director had already established an acquaintance with the local newspaper managing editor. Communication needs good relationships to travel well.

RESEARCH

All fields of major endeavor need extensive research to be effective and current. Professional journals contain a great deal of material on research regarding both social work and child welfare. There are many motives for this, one of which is "publish or perish" policies of universities requiring faculty to publish professional articles to obtain and maintain tenure.

Rebuilding

A nearly universal concern of child welfare personnel is how little the general public and especially elected officials, who control budgets, are aware of their issues and needs. Apparently insufficient emphasis has been given to the value of the potential that research could provide if it were shared with the public. Conceptually that is simple. Changing internal organizational policies might not be as simple.

Consider where research findings currently are published. The next questions are who reads them and how do they use the findings? These questions would make an interesting and very likely a revealing, research study.

When a research study reveals significant information about issues and needs, approaches for dealing with them and results, those findings might have much greater value if they were made public. Public attitudes affect everything child welfare agencies do, and politicians instinctively absorb public attitudes, which tend to influence their support, or lack of support, for services.

If universities gave credit to faculty who produced relevant research findings published in popular publications that are read by the general public, public attitudes could shift in favor of services that demonstrate results. That would require universities to give credit to faculty members for publication in popular publications as well as in professional journals. Greater public understanding of issues also could result in greater public support. Now the public does not have an effective window into our world, but researchers could make it possible.

COLLABORATION

Most effective child welfare services require collaboration with other services. It can enhance the effectiveness of each program, enriching services to clients. It also can increase job satisfaction.

However there can be a fine line between collaboration and abdicating. An example of this is mentioned earlier, (i.e. hiring psychologists to assess a key person in a case and using their findings as an entire case plan). Hiring "counseling" for children needing it, because a worker does not have the skill or time to be able to do it can be abdication. Both these actions dilute the role of child welfare staff, and do not enhance opportunities for developing solid working relationships with their clients. Neither do they help staff to grow.

School social workers, most of whom work with academically challenged children, often share cases with child welfare staff. It is obvious that cooperation between them helps them to work toward the same goals of each child. However various studies have shown that frequently they do not communicate with each other. Casework supervisors in both areas are responsible for making this a work requirement.

Child welfare is not unique in that a clear self-concept is essential for effective collaboration with other organizations. A sound professional social work base can be a major factor in developing clear child welfare self-identity.

An alumni association of adults who had been in foster care can provide strong support for child welfare. Currently a national and many state associations

Rebuilding

exist. They have powerful political influence that can support services for children in care.

Many services outside child welfare impact it heavily, though the connection may not be recognized; for example a special project to enrich day care services for children of mothers who worked in defense plants in Ypsilanti, Michigan during World War II showed remarkably better subsequent functioning of those families and of the children when they became adults. Healthy Start programs that provide supportive visits to new mothers, originated in the Mouri tribe in New Zealand, also was transplanted here. The program shows significant reductions in child abuse. Though less directly related to child welfare, Janet Reno, the Attorney General in the Carter Administration, stated that crime prevention begins with prenatal care. These examples of services, known to strengthen families, illustrate the value of supporting services that greatly benefit families and reduce the need for child welfare services.

INNOVATION

With knowledge expanding exponentially in the world, it is obvious that child welfare also will undergo ongoing change. For child welfare, that presents continuous challenges and opportunities that will require decisions about which approaches must be discarded and when. New types of services are more effective when they are be built on what already is working well.

Some approaches have been introduced and found to be successful, but some of them did not become incorporated throughout the systems. Some examples are as follows.

Specialized family foster care. This program may have different names, such as therapeutic foster care or treatment foster care. Regardless of the name, when the programs are implemented as originally conceived they are powerful. Some basics are well-trained foster parents, professional social work staff monitoring, who have a maximum caseload of ten, and active involvement of parents, in the treatment process where feasible. Previous experience with children by the foster parents in care of children is essential, preferably foster care. Some programs indicated that specialized family foster care is about four times as costly as regular family foster care, but about a fourth of the cost of residential group care. Thus, it is obvious that it is most advantageous when used selectively for children who would otherwise be candidates for group care, with tremendous cost saving. Case assessments can be useful for making such decisions. Outcomes of specialized family foster care generally are superior to group care, sometimes including adoption. Some of these programs are operating, but many more would be beneficial and could greatly reduce the need for expensive group care.

Day treatment. Day treatment can serve populations similar to those in specialized family foster care, ranging from young children with emotional disturbances to delinquent teens. Costs also tend to be similar. The major difference is that children do not sleep in the program, but are picked up early in the day, generally with agency vehicles, and returned home in the evening. Proximity of the program to their homes is significant. The homes also must be sufficiently safe for children to live there at least part time. Programs are similar to residential treatment programs with education being a major program component. Major advantages are that family unity is not fully disrupted making it is easier to keep parents involved and children do not have the stigma of having been removed from their homes.

Homemaker services. Homemaker services, once popular, seem to have nearly disappeared, in spite of being a high yield, low cost program.

Contact families. This preventive program was developed in Sweden for families living "on the edge" and in danger of disintegrating. When a family, usually a single parent family, has difficulty coping and does not have a family support system, this program provides it. Contact parents are recruited much as foster parents are, but do not normally care for the children in their home, excepting for respite care. They serve primarily as a support for the entire family and usually prevent separation of children from their parents. In effect they become supportive family. Friendships that develop often endure indefinitely. Contact families are paid a low wage for the time they spend, apparently similar to our minimum wage. The staff who administered the program report that the cost is about a twelfth as much as regular family foster care and prevents placement of nearly all children in the program.

None of these four programs require special physical facilities. Child welfare may be inflicted with an edifice complex.

Maintaining connections with family members has been developing slowly, but fortunately it is increasing. This includes maintaining ties with siblings in foster care, about 75 percent of them live separately from each other. Lynne Price, founder and president emeritus of Camp to Belong, developed nine summer camps for separated siblings in foster care in the U.S. and other countries, and also assisted a number of states to develop legislation requiring that sibling connections be maintained. These efforts helped to develop nationwide awareness of the value of sibling connections.

The number of children cared for by relatives, especially grandparents, is growing. The Fostering Connections to Success and Increasing Adoptions Act, passed by Congress in October 2008 contains several family related provisions as well as funding. Agencies are required to conduct a diligent search for relatives and other known family members within 30 days of a child's removal. It requires that states make diligent effort to place siblings together. The law requires what should have been standard practice.

According to the Archives of Pediatric and Adolescent Medicine, June 2008, relatives cared for 12 times as many children as are in foster care, with unrelated foster parents and receive better outcomes. It is clear that involvement of families of children in out-of-home care is increasing. Policy changes and staff training are needed to keep up with and implement these changes.

Dispute resolution. Dispute resolution or mediation have been used in child welfare to resolve issues at early stages or at points of strong disagreement. This process has proven itself to be economical and to produce positive outcomes, but has not been incorporated into general practice. Restorative justice programs are similar and are strikingly successful in some juvenile and adult corrections cases.

Reunification and post-adoption services have chronically been in short supply and continue to be at the time of this writing. Each of them can serve to improve case outcomes with savings that are much greater than their cost.

If the past is prologue, it is certain that new program ideas will continue to appear on the scene. Developing new program components requires careful planning and effort, sometimes needing statutorily change. However changes often can be developed with pilot projects initially, to determine if statewide development is feasible. Many states have flexibility to permit pilot test programs without legislative authorization that would be needed for statewide implementation. There are advantages to not using both feet to test the water.

A central value for quality child welfare is that it not be viewed as a child care service but a family support service. Usually the family is one or both birth parents, and when this is not feasible, relatives, adoptive or other substitute parents can become the child's family.

FAMILY FOSTER CARE

This subject fits partially into a number of other categories but deserves consideration in its own right. The mission of child welfare agencies is carried out most directly by foster parents, in concert with agency staff. They are closest to the children and know more about their thinking, feelings and behavior than agency staff do. They also may observe more interactions of children with their parents. Everyone benefits when agency staff involve foster parents as team players.

While the way agencies deal with foster parents varies widely, frequently they report that they are not brought in as part of the agency team in carrying out, or helping to revise, the case plan. A decision to place a child in a home needs to be a mutual decision, with workers fully disclosing what they know about a child before that decision is made by the agency to use the home for a particular child or children, the foster parents are willing to accept the child, and the role of each in implementing the case plan has been made clear. If the plan includes potential for reunification, foster parents must be willing to participate with birth parents, recognizing that concurrent planning must be carried out in some cases. This can sometimes place conflicting emotions on foster parents and must be discussed openly from the outset and when circumstances in cases change. The issue frequently mentioned by foster parents regarding what they need from staff, and frequently lack, is *respect*. Agency staff who expect good performance will show respect and will be respected in return.

Rebuilding

Foster parents sometimes report that agency staff "look down" on them. There is no room for elitism in child welfare.

Payments for regular family foster care only reimburse foster parents for their expenses, at best. This makes it difficult for some foster parents to provide adequate care. Low rates also increase turnover of foster parents, when experience is as vital with them as it is for staff. High turnover is both destructive and costly. It is necessary for agencies to advocate for them.

Both children and foster parents are entitled to advance notice, whenever possible, to prepare children for moves. Removals should not be done abruptly, excepting in emergencies or there is overwhelming evidence of serious abuse in the foster home. Both children and foster parents need preparation time, and sometimes opportunity to grieve. Staff awareness of the grief of foster parents can greatly contribute to foster parent tenure.

Many foster parents also express a need for the opportunity to communicate and collaborate among themselves. Agencies can assist this by encouraging and supporting local and state associations of foster parents. Helping foster parents to develop their own identity can result in better care, and also can enable them to obtain political support for child welfare services.

Most agencies invest heavily in staff training and also in training of foster parents. Some of the content is applicable for both. Training them on that material together not only is economical, but can develop unity and cooperative attitudes that written or separately presented training cannot do. Some foster parents also make effective staff trainers, especially in helping staff understand what foster parents need from them.

With shortages of family foster homes, agencies often redouble recruitment efforts. As important as this is, efforts to increase retention generally produce far greater results, but it is easily overlooked. Retention of foster homes decreases moves for children which can be nearly as traumatic for them as their original removal.

ADOPTION SERVICES

Adoption services, like family foster care, are well established and provide solid services to children and families. In spite of this, there is critical need for improvement in two areas. Post-adoption services are generally lacking. Adoptions have many complications that new adoptive families may not be aware of, especially with children placed after infancy. Skilled counseling often can prevent dissolution of adoptions, with children having to reenter the system with an additional emotionally damaging experience.

Another area of great need is adoption of older teens, although it has increased somewhat in recent years. Teens who have been hurt by families, or who maintain loyalty to birthparents, may be reluctant to be attached to another family. Some teens intensely long to be part of a family but fear adoption because they fear being rejected and hurt again although

Rebuilding

they may not reveal those feelings to caseworkers. However, skilled casework sometimes can find and neutralize these fears. Assumptions that adoption of older teens is inappropriate, or too difficult, also are inappropriate. Adoptions can be arranged at any age.

Child welfare staff are aware that adoptive applicants generally are more interested in adopting infants and some of them are reluctant to adopt teenagers. However at one time a value generally accepted by adoption agencies was that <u>all children are adoptable.</u> As a result, many special needs children and teenagers were adopted, who otherwise would not have been adopted. Positive attitudes make a difference.

STAFF PERSONAL GOALS

Young staff usually begin working with children with the hope that they will positively affect many lives. The practical realities of agency complexity, bureaucracy, personality conflicts, and case complexities all can help to dim that enthusiasm and lead to discouragement. Hopefully there also are rewards that help to keep them going with positive attitudes. But are there methods or principles that a worker can use to deal with that and impact services positively?

First, remember where you came from. Remember what your childhood was like, and what basic values you developed at that time. Everything you learned and will accomplish will in part be based on that foundation, which is *you*.

Second, remember your first jobs, after you receive promotions. Sometimes beginning level jobs are difficult, and workers are glad to be able to rise

Because Kids Are Worth It!

to levels above them. That presents a test of your professional ethics. Remember then that the agency mission is carried out most directly by the people you left behind. What you can do to enhance their effort increases the effectiveness of the agency in carrying out its mission.

Third, never put your personal interests <u>too far</u> ahead of the mission of the agency. Everyone does that at times, and a certain amount of self-interest and gratification are essential for continued productivity. Just be careful that they do not dominate you and become your reason for being there.

Albert Einstein put this concept into perspective with a simple statement. "If you wish to have a happy life, attach yourself to a goal, not to people or things." Another formula that may be helpful is "Keep one eye on your goal, and one eye on your feet."

CONCLUSION

Quality has many factors, some requiring money, but some do not, such as commitment, clear focus at all levels, cooperation, good communication and sensitivity to client needs, a sense of humor and sometimes simple common sense. Every day struggles may seem overwhelming. Then it can be difficult to reach for excellence. However, excellence is available more than we normally believe it is. Even when work is difficult, with effort and teamwork some quality may be available, increasing both job successes and satisfaction.

Now at the end of this effort, it may be time to look back to the beginning. In 1954 eight of us had just

Rebuilding

---

finished one year of graduate school and were about to go to our first jobs as child welfare workers. We spent a few days in the Lansing state office for orientation. Our school year had been financed by a "work study plan" with funds provided by the Children's Bureau. One of our meetings was with Willard J. Maxey, director of what then was the Public Welfare Department. A statement he made was significant because it helped to put our responsibility into focus and also clarified that it is reasonable to expect to be able to work with a margin of error. Hopefully it can be useful now with any new staff and perhaps it is even more valuable for administrators at any level as an effective way to perceive their role and communicate it to subordinates.

"When you go to your child welfare jobs in those rural areas, you will make mistakes. When you do, I will hear about them. But if I don't hear about them I will assume that you are not doing anything, because anyone who does things makes mistakes. It will be necessary for you to make decisions concerning children. So go ahead and make them <u>because kids are worth it</u>."

A child is a person who is going to carry on what you have started.

He is going to sit where you are sitting, and when you are gone, attend to the things that you think are important.

You may adopt all the policies you please, but how they are carried out depends on him.

He will assume control of your cities, states and nations.

He is going to move in and take over your churches, schools, universities and corporations.

The fate of humanity is in his (or her) hands.

Abraham Lincoln

About the Author

Jake Terpstra is a social worker. He graduated from Calvin College in Grand Rapids, Michigan and the University of Michigan, where he received a Master's degree in Social Work.

His career of more than a half century, began as a child welfare caseworker in a rural area for the Michigan Department of Public Welfare, now the Department of Human Services. Then he administered the Washtenaw County Juvenile Detention Home and following that, a private residential treatment program for children. He next went to the Lansing central office of the state agency and administered the program for licensing child welfare services in Michigan.

After his statewide experience, Mr. Terpstra was appointed by the U.S Children's Bureau as a national specialist in state licensing of child welfare services. With government downsizing, he was asked to also serve as the government specialist for group care of children and for family foster care. These responsibilities included establishing and monitoring federal grants in those specialty areas and monitoring the grants.

His responsibilities also were open ended, responding to child welfare administrators throughout the country, to provide training, consultation or assistance with conference planning. Sometimes consultation included legislators. He initiated the National Association of State Foster Care Managers and edited a national newsletter on state licensing. During this time he wrote many articles on subjects he believed had not been adequately addressed. After retirement he served on two agency boards of directors, county and state child welfare committees, a foster care review board and continued to provide consultation.

His experience began as a caseworker, then moved to administrative positions with statewide and national responsibility that included contacts with thousands of people working in child welfare throughout this country and also in other countries. He recognized that at all levels the core values of child welfare services are basic even though different methods are required. His writing this book is an attempt to share those experiences and observations with anyone interested in child welfare service, about what it is and what it could be.

Acknowledgements

Gwen Morgan, Senior Fellow, Wheelock College, Boston, who has done extensive research and writing on children's issues, carefully reviewed and commented on manuscript drafts.

Ed Sites, professor of social work at the University of Pennsylvania also was the director of pre-service and in-service public child welfare education in Pennsylvania. He shared his knowledge about effective statewide public and private education practices on both graduate and undergraduate, and the positive effect they have on child welfare services.

Joan Zlotnik, staff member of the National Association of Social Workers, always up-to-date on national child welfare legislation, freely shared that information.

Joe Woodard, formerly with the U.S. Administration for Children and Families, still serves as the "numbers man," of both children in the system and money.

Jeni Hoekstra, friend, who understands grammar as well as she does computers.

My wife Marty, for her supportive patience.